MONTH-BY-MONTH
PHONICS
FOR FIRST GRADE
SYSTEMATIC, MULTILEVEL INSTRUCTION

by
Patricia M. Cunningham
and
Dorothy P. Hall

Project Coordinator
Joyce Kohfeldt
I.E.S.S., Kernersville, NC

Senior Editor
Chris McIntyre

Illustrators
Kathryn Mitter
Pam Thayer

Month-by-Month Phonics for First Grade
by Patricia M. Cunningham and Dorothy P. Hall

This book is dedicated to first grade teachers everywhere and especially those teachers who have shared ideas with us and whose superb teaching inspired the writing of this book. There are many whose names we have forgotten—or, in some cases, never knew. But we learned from the questions they posed and the solutions they offered. Particular thanks goes to the following teachers with whom we have worked most closely during the past ten years:

Kellie Alston	Betty Hayashi	Sonja Patrick
Yolander Bailey	Deidre Howie	Heidi Reckord
Denise Boger	Paula Jordan	Adrienne Reynolds
Marie Daniel	Christine Joyner	Judy Seaver
Margaret Defee	Jan Kornelis	Amanda Sieg
Glenda Greene	Janet Leonard	Tammy West
Cindy Harper	Athlene Lockhart	Linda Wigley
	Susie Marion	
	Gay Moss	

Senior Editor
Chris McIntyre

Illustrators
Kathryn Mitter
Pam Thayer

Project Coordinator
Joyce Kohfeldt
I.E.S.S., Kernersville, NC

ISBN 0-88724-397-5

TABLE OF CONTENTS

INTRODUCTION

Phonics is the current "hot topic." Everyone is talking about phonics, and everyone has an opinion about what should be taught, when and how. Phonics *is* an important part of beginning literacy instruction, but phonics is not all that matters. In fact, children who come to school with limited reading experiences and who are taught in a "phonics first, phonics only" approach often get the idea that reading is "sounding out words"! You do have to figure out words, but reading is not figuring out words and "sounding good." Figuring out words is the means to the end of understanding, learning, thinking, and enjoying.

It seems foolish as we approach a new millennium to have to point out this basic fact. Decades of research support the idea that children need phonics but that children who are taught phonics only until they "get it" don't suddenly get transformed into eager, meaning-seeking, strategic readers (Cunningham, 1995). Good readers do know phonics and they use phonics to figure out some words. But good readers also recognize the most frequent words instantly as sight words and they use context to check that what they are reading and the words they have figured out make sense.

Teaching *all* children to read is essential and can be done, but it will never happen with a "just teach 'em phonics" curriculum. Children do not all learn in the same way. Some children do learn to read by reading, others learn to read through writing. Some children learn sight words very quickly and know words forever after just reading them once or twice. These fast word learners do not do much decoding while they read because they do not need to!

The word *balance* is currently in danger of extinction from overuse. But the concept of balance is and will remain a critically-important idea. To us, balance in literacy instruction is like a balanced diet. We make sure that children eat from the basic food groups because each group is important to growth. We decide how much of each group should be included in a balanced diet and these amounts change as people grow older. We do not try to decide which of the basic groups is best nor do we go through phases in which "experts" recommend that children only eat from one group!

To become good readers, children need a balanced literacy diet. The basic Four Blocks of balanced literacy instruction are: Shared/ Guided Reading, Self-Selected Reading, Writing, and Working with Words. In numerous successful primary classrooms in which we have worked, teachers divide their language-arts time each day into these Four Blocks, each lasting 30-40 minutes each. In Four-Blocks classrooms, children spend one fourth of their time in Guided Reading of books and stories chosen and guided by the teacher. They spend another fourth of their time in Self-Selected Reading where they choose what they want to read. Another fourth of their time is spent Writing. Another fourth is spent Working with Words, including sight words, phonics, and spelling.

This book provides month-by-month activities for one quarter of a well-balanced literacy diet—the Working With Words Block. When combined with the other three essential Blocks (Shared/Guided Reading, Self-Selected Reading, and Writing), all children's literacy skills grow at their optimum rates.

Many years of working in Four-Blocks classrooms have convinced us that each of the four components is equally important and that, in spite of what comes in and out of fashion, children develop best as readers and writers when their daily instruction provides this balanced literacy diet. We invite you to read the Overview of the Four-Blocks program at the end of this book and use your own experience with teaching and children to decide if you are satisfied with the balanced literacy diet you are providing your first graders.

Finally, as you begin this book, we would like you to think about the kind of phonics instruction you will find here. For a long time, the phonics debate centered on whether to teach using a synthetic or an analytic approach. Synthetic approaches generally teach children to go letter-by-letter, assigning a pronunciation to each letter and then blending individual letters together. Analytic approaches teach rules (when an **e** is added to the end of a word, it makes the preceding vowel long). Brain research, however, suggests that the brain is a pattern detector, not a rule applier, and that, while we look at single letters, we are not assigning them sounds; rather we are looking at clusters of letters and considering the letter patterns we know (Adams, 1990).

When good readers first see a phonetically regular word (such as **swoop** or **quest**), they immediately assign it a pronunciation. This happens so quickly that readers are often unaware that they have not seen the word before and that they had to "figure it out." Successful decoding occurs when the brain recognizes a familiar spelling pattern. **Swoop** and **quest** could each be quickly decoded or spelled by using the similar known words **loop**, **troop**, **best**, or **west**. This process of using other words with similar patterns to figure out the unfamiliar word is commonly called **decoding by analogy** (Cunningham, 1995).

The phonics activities in this book are consistent with the brain research that supports the idea that decoding and spelling are not accomplished by sounding out words letter-by-letter or by rules. Rather, children learn from the beginning how to use patterns in words they know to decode and spell hundreds of other words.

In addition to phonics patterns, the book provides activities so that children develop a store of instant words—high-frequency words they can instantly decode and spell. Activities are also included to make sure that readers learn the important strategy of cross-checking—checking a word they have figured out to make sure it makes sense. We hope you find these activities healthy and tasty additions to the balanced literacy diet you are providing your fledgling readers and writers.

AUGUST/SEPTEMBER

It's the first day of first grade! The children bustle in, most a little nervous and shy, lugging their carefully-chosen book bags and lunch boxes. Little as they are, they know that this is an important milestone. They are in first grade. They are growing up. They are going to learn to read!

The teachers are excited, too, and most, even after years of teaching first grade, are still a little nervous and apprehensive. Looking at those eager little bodies, they wonder if the "miracle" will happen again this year. Because it really is a miracle (and a miracle performed at no other grade!)—Taking these 20-30 eager, excited little children and transforming almost all of them into readers in nine short months—just the amount of time their bodies grew in their mothers' wombs!

How does this miracle happen? How do so many children, most of whom can't read when they burst through the doors of first grade, learn to turn the little black marks on paper into stories that make them laugh and facts that fascinate them? Most first-grade teachers will tell you that it happens very gradually and that it requires not only faith but a lot of hard work! To a great extent, the miracle depends on what happens during the first month of school. All children come to school expecting that they will learn to read. The "big people" they know can read and, now that they are in first grade, they will be able to read too!

The activities we do with children during the first month of first grade need to develop a wide range of concepts and strategies. We define such activities as **multilevel. A multilevel activity is one where there are *multiple things to be learned* and *multiple ways for children to move forward*.**

By the end of the first 4-6 weeks, you will have introduced the following:

- choral and echo reading
- using students' names to make letter, sound, and word observations
- retelling, rereading, and acting out a story from a book read to the class
- sequencing some sentences, words, and letters to match story text
- making rhymes and playing with words to develop phonemic awareness
- using songs and rhymes to learn the letters of the alphabet
- using the classroom to explore beginning sounds for each letter

The goal of the first-month activities presented in this chapter is to ensure that the confidence the children bring on the first day remains intact (and is even enhanced). All children come to first grade expecting to learn to read. At the end of the first month, all children should know that they *can* read!

In this chapter, we will describe some activities for the first 4-6 weeks of school which accomplish the goals of developing critical concepts and strategies, while simultaneously convincing all children that they are becoming readers.

Now we know that our use of the word *all* has most of you shaking your heads and wondering if we have seen the first-grade classes in your school! While we haven't seen all the first-grade classes there are, we have seen enough to know what you are worrying about.

Some of those eager young bodies bustling through your classroom door don't know a single letter or sound! Many can't read a single word—including their own name! Some can't track print and a few don't even know that print is the funny little black marks you read. They think you read the pictures!

Mixed in with these "eager but less experienced" children are children who can't read yet but have developed a lot of these critical-to-success reading concepts. In most classrooms, there are also a few children who come to first grade already reading quite well.

What can you do during the first 4-6 weeks of school which will meet the needs of this wide range of entering literacy levels found in almost every first-grade? We will try to answer these questions in this chapter.

At the end of this chapter, we will consider again these different levels of children and ask you to decide for yourself:

1. Do the children who enter "without a clue" have some things they can read and be convinced that they are learning to read?

2. Can the children who come to school ready to read (but are not actually reading) be started on their way to becoming readers?

3. Can the children (and the parents of the children) who come already reading be satisfied that they are making progress and not just marking time waiting for everyone else to catch up?

These are not easy goals—but they are the real goals! Children come to us at all different literacy levels and they must all sense that they are making progress if their eagerness and excitement is to sustain them through the hard work of learning to read.

GETTING TO KNOW YOU

To begin our multilevel journey toward literacy for all, we will start with what is most important to five- and six-year olds—them! Most first-grade teachers begin their year with some get-acquainted activities. As part of these get-acquainted activities, they often have a special child each day. In addition to learning about each child, you can focus attention on the special child's name and use the name to develop some important understandings about words and letters.

Preparation

To prepare for these get-acquainted activities, write all the children's first names (with initials for last names if two names are the same) with a permanent marker on sentence strips. Cut the strips so that long names have long strips and short names have short strips. Let the children watch you write their names and have them help you spell their names if they can.

We want the children to watch and "think" as the names are being written and they usually will because they are so interested in themselves–and each other. Their attention for anything, however, diminishes after 15-20 minutes, so if you have a large class, you may want to write the names in two different sessions.

After writing each name, display it in a pocket chart or on a wall or board. As you put each name up, comment on letters shared by certain names or on other common features:

> "Rasheed's name starts with an **R** just like Robert's."

> "Bo's name has only two letters."

> "We have two girls named Ashley, so I will have to put the letter **M** after this name so that we will know it is for Ashley Martin."

Once you have displayed the names, ask volunteers to come and find a name they can read. Many children will read their own and almost everyone will remember **Bo**!

"Special Child" of the Day

Tell the children that each day, one of them will be the special child. Let them know that you are going to put all the names in a box and you will draw a name from the box each day to randomly determine the special child. Tell the children what the special child will get to do each day. Some teachers crown that child king or queen, let the child lead the line, decide what game to play for P.E., sit in a special chair to greet visitors, pass things out, take messages to the office, etc. Do keep in mind that whatever you do for the first, you must do for all the rest, so make sure you can sustain whatever you start. (Remember the, "Don't do anything the first month of marriage you don't want to do the whole rest of your married life," advice many get but ignore!) Each day, reach into the box and draw out a name. This child becomes the special child and the focus of many literacy activities. For our example, we will assume that **David** is the first name pulled from the box.

Interviewing and Shared Writing

20 min.

Have David come up and sit in a special chair and appoint the rest of the class reporters. The job of the reporters is to interview David and find out what he likes to eat, play, do after school, etc. Does he have brothers? sisters? cats? dogs? mice? Decide on a certain number of questions (5-7) and call on different children to ask the questions.

After the interview, write your "newspaper article" on this special child using a shared writing format in which the children give suggestions and you and they decide what to say first, last, etc. Record this on a chart while the children watch. The chart should be no more than 5-6 sentences long and the sentences should not be too complex because these articles about each "special child" will form some of the first material most children will be able to read. The interview and the writing of the chart can be completed in the 20-minute attention span if the teacher limits the number of questions and takes the lead in the writing of the article. This first activity for each child—interviewing and shared writing of the article—develops crucial oral language skills and helps children see how writing and reading occur.

Shared Reading of the Charts

20 min.

The second activity is the reading of David's chart. This takes place later in the day and again, does not take more than twenty minutes. On the first day, you will only have one chart to read. **Lead the children to read it chorally several times and let volunteers come and read each sentence. Guide their hands so that they are tracking print as they read.** Most teachers display each chart for five days and then take the chart down to make room for a new one. That way, there are only five charts in the room at any one time but every chart gets read and reread on five different days. Be sure to save the charts (roll them up and store them safely) because they will be used in some of the October activities.

Many teachers also write or type the chart and (after all the children have had their special days and been interviewed) compile a class book containing each article, often along with a picture of each child. Each child then has one night to take the book home so that the family can get to know the whole class.

Katherine Gardzalla

Katherine Gardzalla is 5 years old.
She will be 6 in two days.
Her favorite drink is apple juice.
Her favorite music is rock and roll.
Mrs. Stokes is her favorite teacher.
Katherine Gardzalla is a good student.

Focusing on the Name

Now focus everyone's attention on the child's name. Point to the word **David** on the sentence strip and develop children's understanding of jargon by pointing out that this **word** is David's name. Tell them that it takes many **letters** to write the word **David**, and let them help you count the letters. Say the letters **D-a-v-i-d**, and have the children chant with you cheerleader-style. (We call this cheering for David, and he loves it!) Point out that the word **David begins** and **ends** with the **same** letter. Explain that the **d** looks different because one is a **capital D** and the other is a **small d**–or **uppercase/lowercase**–whatever jargon you use.

The jargon in the above paragraph is in bold to emphasize important print words with which children must be familiar as they learn to read.

Take another sentence strip and have children watch as you write **David**. Have them chant the spelling of the letters with you. Cut the letters apart and mix them up. Let several children come and arrange the letters in just the right order so that they spell **David**. Have the other children chant to check that the order is correct.

Display David's name on a bulletin board reserved for the names of the special children or make it the first word you add to your Word Wall (lots more about the Word Wall in the October chapter).

Writing

The final activity to do with each name allows the children to focus on the name by writing it. Notice that all the learning modes are being used with each name. **They are looking (visual), they are chanting (auditory), and they are writing (kinesthetic)!** Give each child a sheet of drawing paper and have the child write the name in large letters on one side of the paper. Model at the board how to write each letter as the children write on their papers (but do not expect their writing to look just like yours and resist the temptation to correct what they write). Early in the year children who haven't written much will reverse letters and make them in funny ways. The important understanding is that names are words, that words can be written, and that it takes lots of letters to write them. **We are giving them a kinesthetic way to focus on the word and while we model correct handwriting we do not, at this point, expect correct letter formation from everyone.**

After each child writes the name, she turns her paper over and draws a picture of David on the other side of the drawing paper. At the end of the day, David takes all the pictures home!

After students have written several names, you might allow them to try writing one of the chart sentences or one of their own sentences about the child of the day. Children who are unable to write a sentence can enjoy trying to write the name of the child of the day and drawing his picture.

Comparing Names

15 min.

Imagine that it is the next day and the name pulled from the box is **Catherine**. She has been interviewed and a chart article written. Choral and individual readings of her chart (along with David's chart) have been done. It is now time to focus student attention on the sentence strip with Catherine's name. Say the letters in **Catherine** and have the children chant them by cheering for Catherine. Help the children to count the letters and decide which letter is **first**, **last**, etc. Point out that **Catherine** has two **e**'s and they look exactly the **same** because both are **small (lowercase) e**'s. Write **Catherine** on a second sentence strip and cut it into letters. Have children arrange the letters to spell **Catherine**, using the first sentence strip as their model.

Put **Catherine** on the bulletin board (or wall) and compare the name to **David**. Which name has the most letters? How many more letters are in **Catherine** than in **David**? Does **Catherine** have any of the same letters as **David**?

The next name to be chosen is **Robert**. Do all the usual activities, including interviewing; chart writing; reading of Robert's, Catherine's and David's charts; cheering for Robert by chanting the letters in his name; and writing his name again, cutting it into letters and rearranging the letters to spell his name. Be sure to note the two **r**'s and talk about why they look different.

As you put **Robert** on the board or Word Wall, compare it to both **David** and **Catherine**. **Robert** has an **e** and **Catherine** has two **e**'s. **Robert** and **Catherine** each have a **t**. **Robert** doesn't have any of the same letters that **David** has. Robert's name has six letters—more than **David** but fewer than **Catherine**.

Mike is chosen next. When you have a one-syllable name with which there are many rhymes (**Pat, Fran, Joe, Sue**, etc.), seize the opportunity to help the children listen for words that rhyme with that name. Pair the name with other words, some of which rhyme with **Mike** and others which do not:

Mike/ball	Mike/bike	Mike/cook
Mike/hike	Mike/like	Mike/chair

If the pairs rhyme, everyone should point at Mike and whisper, "Mike." If not, they should shake their heads and frown.

Variant Consonant Sounds

5 min.

Let's suppose we are comparing names and the special child of the day is Cindy. **Catherine** and **Cindy** both begin with the letter **c**, but begin with different sounds. Have Catherine and Cindy stand on opposite sides of you. Write their names above them on the chalkboard. Have the children say **Catherine** and **Cindy** several times–drawing out the first sound each time. Help them to understand that some letters can have more than one sound and that the names **Catherine** and **Cindy** show us that. Tell the class that you are going to say some words, all of which begin with the letter **c**. Some of these words sound like **Catherine** at the beginning and some sound like **Cindy**. Say some words such as the following and have the children say them with you:

cat	celery	candy
cookies	city	cereal

For each word, have students point to Catherine or Cindy to show which sound they hear. Once they have decided, write each word on the chalkboard under the name **Catherine** or **Cindy**.

Continue to choose names each day, and as you add each to your board or wall, help the children notice whatever they can about letter-sound relationships. The names your children have will determine what you will help the children to notice.

If you don't have names such as **Catherine** and **Cindy**, you would not point out the two sounds of **c** this early in the year, but if you do, you have to help the children understand that some letters have more than one sound or they will get confused. Children do notice things we don't point out, and if we just teach **c** as having the sound in **Catherin**e, **cat**, and **candy**, Cindy may be looking at her name tag and wondering why she can't hear the same beginning sound! **English is not a one-letter—one-sound language. There are relationships, but they are complex. We must help children see how letters represent sounds, but if we make it simpler than it really is, some children are apt to notice the contradiction and get confused and maybe come to the dangerous conclusion that "there isn't any system and pattern to these letters and sounds."**

So, if you have a **Joseph** and a **Julio** or a **Sheila** and a **Sam**, don't be afraid to discuss the variant sounds. Point out that it is the **sh** in **Sheila** that gives **s** its different sound. **Most of the children who are just beginning to learn about how letters and sounds are related would not need to know this. But those who were already reading when they came to first grade probably know the single-letter sounds and are ready to realize that some letter combinations have different sounds.**

Finally, as you get to about the halfway point in adding the names, let the children take charge of noticing the similarities and differences between the names. Instead of pointing out as you add **Rasheed** that the name starts with the same letter and sound as **Robert** and the name has two **e**'s and it ends with a **d** like **David**, ask the children:

> "What do you notice about the letters and sounds in Rasheed's name and the other names on our wall?"

There is a system and a pattern to the way letters in English represent sounds. Our instruction should point out these patterns. Children who see a new word and ask themselves how that new word is like the other words they know can discover many patterns on their own.

How Getting to Know You Is Multilevel

Now that you have an example to relate to, we want you to think about how the Getting to Know You activity is composed of *multilevel activities*.

What about the children who enter school with almost no understanding of what reading and writing are and how they work? After participating in the interviewing, shared writing, name board activities, and writing of each child's name, almost all these "eager but less experienced" children are able to:

- track print—starting at the right, pointing to one word at a time, and making the return sweep to the left

- point to just one word and just one letter, to the first word in a sentence and the first letter in a word, showing they have learned important print jargon and concepts

- read at least five (and usually many more) of the names of their classmates

- write many of the names in a fashion that can be read by others (even though handwriting may leave much to be desired)

- name some of the letters of the alphabet

- demonstrate some understanding that letters and sounds are related by telling you some words (names) that begin with different letters.

While these children are developing the critical foundation for moving into literacy, other children who come to school prepared but not reading are actually learning to read and write. These children can:

- read and write the names of almost all their classmates

- name all the letters that occur in these names

- look for patterns and relationships between letters and sounds

- read the chart articles about themselves

- read a lot of the words in the Special Child Charts about students in class.

Finally, we must not forget the children who come to school already reading. What do they learn through the Getting to Know You activities? These fast learners, as we should expect, make the most progress. They can:

- read all the chart articles fluently

- write a several-sentence article about a classmate

- read and spell words such as **the, in, he, she, boy, girl,** and **likes**

- understand that letters can have a variety of sounds depending on what letters follow them

- learn, on their own, patterns not yet taught because they are used to looking at new words and trying to figure out why the letters do what they do.

Getting to Know You is a truly multi-level activity. Its use in the first 4-6 weeks of school accomplishes the goals of moving all levels of children forward and maintaining their enthusiasm and confidence.

SHARED READING OF PREDICTABLE BIG BOOKS

Another popular success-oriented activity for the first 4-6 weeks of first grade is the reading of predictable big books. Since this is a much better known and commonly-used activity, we will give it less page space but will point out some ways to enhance its multilevel potential. For our example, we have chosen the ever popular *Hattie and the Fox*, by Mem Fox (Simon & Schuster, 1988). In this book, Hattie the hen notices something in the bushes:

> "Goodness gracious me! I can see a nose in the bushes!"

The other animals respond:

> "Good grief," said the goose.
>
> "Well, well," said the pig.
>
> "Who cares?" said the sheep.
>
> "So what?" said the horse.
>
> "What next?" said the cow.

As the story continues, Hattie sees a nose and two eyes in the bushes, then a nose, two eyes, and two ears. Next two legs appear, followed by a body and two more legs. As Hattie announces each new sighting, the other animals respond with the same lack of concern. But when Hattie announces it is a fox, the other animals respond:

> "Oh, no!" said the goose.
>
> "Dear me!" said the pig.
>
> "Oh, dear!" said the sheep.
>
> "Oh, help!" said the horse.
>
> But the cow said "MOO!"

This frightens the fox away and the animals go on about their business.

Read and Talk About the Book

As with any book, the first and second reading of a big book should be strictly focused on the meaning and enjoyment of the book. This book has delightful illustrations and children will enjoy the suspense of watching the fox emerge.

15 min.

Encourage the children to join in the reading in any of a variety of ways. For a book like *Hattie and the Fox*, children will almost naturally want to say the responses of the animals and join Hattie in naming the body parts of the fox as she sees them. You might also "echo read" the book by reading one line at a time and letting the children repeat it. Some teachers like to have the class make a tape recording in which the teacher reads some parts and the whole class or groups of children read other parts or some of the characters' lines. Children delight in going to the listening center and listening to themselves reading the book!

Act It Out

Young children are natural actors. They pretend and act out all kinds of things. They don't need props or costumes, but you may want to make some simple line drawings of the characters on construction paper or tagboard. (Drawings done for Hattie and for the Fox can include several versions for the fox; each drawing can show a little bit more of the fox emerging from the bushes). Punch holes in the top of each picture, tie each end of a length of yarn through the holes, and let children wear the pictures around their necks so everyone will know which characters they are! Act out the story several times, letting everyone have a chance to be one of the animals or a version of the fox. Read the part that is not repetitive and let children in the audience read with you.

Matching Sentence Strips to the Book

15 min.

Write some of the sentences, such as the repeated responses of the animals, on sentence strips. Let children put them in the right order by matching them to the same sentences in the book and arranging them in a pocket chart. Have children read from the sentence strips.

Increase the difficulty of the matching activity by having students arrange *words* to make *sentences*. Choose two or three sentence strips copied from a single page of the book and let the children watch you cut the sentence strips into words. Mix up the words and have them recreate the book page from the words. Children enjoy manipulating the words and it is excellent practice for left-to right, top-to-bottom print tracking.

Letter and Word Observations

Choose some sentences from the book such as the following:

"Good grief," said the goose.

"Well, well," said the pig.

"Who cares?" said the sheep.

"So what?" said the horse.

"What next?" said the cow.

Ask the children to look at these sentences and have them point out what they notice. Children will notice a variety of things depending on their level. These will probably include:

"**Good**, **grief**, and **goose** each begin with a **g**."

"**Pig** has a **g** too, but it is at the end."

"**Said** is in every sentence—five times!"

"**The** is also there five times!"

"**What** is there two times."

"The **What** in the last sentence has a capital **W**."

"All the sentences have these (pointing to quotation marks) things."

Whatever the children notice should be accepted and praised. Also ask more questions, such as the following:

"Does anyone know what these marks (point to the question marks) are called? Why are they there?"

and offer explanations such as:

"These are called question marks, and they are there because the animals are asking questions."

Once a book has been read, enjoyed, reread, and acted out by the class, most children will be able to read (or pretend read) most of the book by themselves. This early "I Can Read" confidence is critical to first graders, and the shared book experience as described in this section is a wonderful way to foster such confidence.

How Shared Reading Is Multilevel

The Shared Reading activities are multilevel in many of the same ways that the Getting to Know You activities are. There are many different things for children to notice when they are working with a book.

Children coming to first grade who are already reading will:
- learn more words
- begin to notice the similarities and differences in words

Children with little print experience will:
- learn what reading is
- begin to develop their concepts of print
- learn a few words
- develop the desire to learn to read
- gain the confidence that they *are* learning to read!

Here are some other favorite books which, because of their predictable nature, can be read by many children and are good confidence-builders:

Big Books

The Bear Escape, by Gare Thompson. (Steck-Vaughn, 1997)

The Biggest Sandwich Ever, by Jeffrey Stoodt. (Steck-Vaughn, 1997)

Five Little Monkeys. (Mondo, 1995)

Franklin In the Dark, by Paulette Bourgeois. (Scholastic, 1986)

I Went Walking, by Sue Williams. (Harcourt Brace, 1990)

If You Give a Mouse a Cookie, by Laura Joffe Numeroff. (Harper & Row, 1985)

It Didn't Frighten Me, by Janet Goss and Jerome Harste. (Mondo, 1995)

Little Red and the Wolf, by Gare Thompson. (Steck-Vaughn, 1997)

Oh No! by Bronwen Scarffe. (Mondo, 1994)

Time for Bed, by Mem Fox. (Celebration Press, 1993.)

When Goldilocks Went to the House of the Bears. (Mondo, 1995)

Zoo-looking, by Mem Fox. (Mondo, 1995)

Small Books

Are You There, Bear? by Ron Maris. (Puffin, 1986)

Button Buttons, by Rozanne Lanczac Williams. (Creative Teaching Press, 1994)

Choose Me! by Sharon Siamon. (Gage, 1987)

I Can Read, by Rozanne Lanczac Williams. (Creative Teaching Press, 1994)

I Can Write, by Rozanne Lanczac Williams. (Creative Teaching Press, 1994)

I See Colors, by Rozanne Lanczac Williams. (Creative Teaching Press, 1994)

Jump, Frog, Jump! by Robert Kalan. (Greenwillow Books, 1981)

When I Grow Up, by Babs Bell Hajdusiewicz. (Dominie Press, 1996)

Where's Spot? by Eric Hill. (Putnam, 1980)

Who Reads? by Betty Aynaga. (Dominie Press, 1996)

CHANTING RHYMES AND SHARING RHYMING BOOKS

Children and rhymes just go together. Children love rhymes. They love to chant them and sing them and make them up. Most first-grade teachers have an amazing store of rhymes and fingerplays which just go with their units throughout the seasons.

Doing rhymes with children, however, is not just for fun! **Rhyming activities develop one of the most critical concepts for success in beginning reading—phonemic awareness.** Have you listened to kindergartners on the playground when they want to tease one another? What do they say? Often you hear chants such as *Billy is silly*; *Saggy, baggy Maggie*, etc. **Making rhymes and playing with words is one of the most reliable indicators that children are getting control of language. They are becoming aware of words and sounds and can manipulate these to express themselves—and to impress others!**

This ability to manipulate sounds is called *phonemic awareness*, and children's levels of phonemic awareness are very highly correlated with their success in beginning reading. Phonemic awareness develops through a series of stages during which children first become aware that language is made up of individual words, that words are made up of syllables, and that syllables are made up of phonemes. It is important to note here that this is not the "jargon" children learn. Most six- or seven-year-olds cannot tell you there are three **syllables** in **dinosaur** and one **syllable** in **Rex**. What they can do is clap out the beats in **dinosaur** and the one beat in **Rex**. Likewise, they cannot tell you that the first **phoneme** in **mice** is **m**, but they can tell you what you would have if you took the **"m-m-m"** off **mice—ice.**

Children develop **phonemic awareness** as a result of exposure to oral and written language. Nursery rhymes, chants, and Dr. Seuss books usually play a large role in this development. As you are doing rhymes with children, remember that you are not just doing something you and they enjoy, you are also developing their understanding that words are made up of sounds and that sounds can be changed to make different words. **Only when children realize that words can be changed and how changing a sound changes the word are they able to profit from instruction in letter-sound relationships.**

Using Rhyming Books

30 min.

There are many wonderful rhyming books, but because of their potential to develop phonemic awareness, two deserve special mention. Along with other great rhyming books, Dr. Seuss wrote *There's a Wocket in My Pocket* (Random House, 1974). In this book, all kinds of Seussian creatures are found in various places. In addition to the wocket in the pocket, there is a vug under the rug, a nureau in the bureau and a yottle in the bottle! After several readings, children delight in chiming in to provide the name of the nonsensical creature lurking in each place. After reading the book a few times, it would be fun to decide what creatures might be lurking in your classroom. Let children make up the names of the creatures and accept whatever they say as long as the names rhyme with the objects:

"There's a **pock** on our **clock**!"

"There's a **zindow** looking in our **window**!"

"There's a **zencil** on my **pencil**!"

Another wonderful rhyming book for phonemic awareness is *The Hungry Thing*, by Jan Slepian and Ann Seidler (Scholastic, 1988). In this book, a large, friendly dinosaur-looking creature (You have to see him to love him!) comes to town, wearing a sign that says,

"Feed Me."

When asked what he would like to eat, he responds,

"Shmancakes."

After much deliberation, a clever little boy offers him some pancakes. The Hungry Thing eats them all up and demands,

"Tickles."

Again, after much deliberation the boy figures out he wants pickles. As the story continues, it becomes obvious that The Hungry Thing wants specific foods and he asks for them by saying words that rhyme with what he wants. He asks for feetloaf and gobbles down the meatloaf. For desert, he wants hookies and gollipops!

> Children love listening to and chiming in with both *There's a Wocket in My Pocket* and *The Hungry Thing*. If the reading of these books is followed up by activities allowing the children to create silly rhyming words, their phonemic awareness development is greatly enhanced.

If you wish to complement the class reading of *The Hungry Thing* with a display, consider making a poster-size Hungry Thing, complete with his sign that reads **Feed Me** on one side and **Thank You!** on the other. Armed with real foods (or pictures of foods), the children can try to feed The Hungry Thing. Of course, he won't eat the food unless it is offered with a rhyming name. If they offer him spaghetti, they have to say,

"Want some **bagetti**?" (or **zagetti**, or **ragetti**—any silly word that rhymes with spaghetti!)

To feed him brownies, they have to offer him **fownies** or **mownies**!

Additional Rhyming Books

There are lots of wonderful rhyming books. A few of our favorites for first-graders are:

Ape in a Cape, by Fritz Eichenberg. (Harcourt Brace, 1952)

Jake Baked the Cake, by B. G. Hennessey. (Viking, 1990)

Pretend You're a Cat, by J. Marzollo. (Dial, 1990)

SINGING THE ALPHABET SONG AND SHARING ALPHABET BOOKS

"The Alphabet Song" has been sung by generations of children. Children enjoy it, and it does seem to give them a sense of all the letters and a framework in which to put new letters as they learn them. Many children come to school already able to sing "The Alphabet Song." Let them sing it and teach it to everyone else. Once the children can sing the song, you may want to point to alphabet cards (usually found above the chalkboard) as they sing. Children enjoy "being the alphabet" as they line up to go somewhere. Simply pass out laminated alphabet cards—one to each child, leftovers to the teacher—and let the children sing the song slowly as each child lines up. Be sure to hand out the cards randomly so that no children are repeatedly assigned the **A** or the **Z**.

There are also lots of wonderful alphabet books to read and enjoy. Many of these will fit into your themes or units. **Research shows that simple books with not too many words on a page and pictures that most of the children recognize are the most helpful to children in building their letter-sound and letter-name knowledge** (Routman, 1988; DeFord, Lyons, & Pinnell, 1991). Once the book has been read and reread several times, children will enjoy reading it during their self-selected reading time. It is very important that children have time to choose and read books each day, and simple alphabet books which have been read together can also be read by individual children who are unable to read books with more text.

Alphabet Book List

Here are a few alphabet books that meet our "not too many words, familiar pictures, kids love to read them" criteria:

The Accidental Zucchini, by Max Grover. (Browndeer Press, 1993)

The Alphabet Tale, by Jan Garten. (Random House, 1964)

Chicka Chicka Boom Boom, by Bill Martin, Jr., and John Archambault. (Simon & Schuster, 1989)

Chicka Chicka Sticka Sticka, by Bill Martin, Jr., and John Archambault. (Simon & Schuster, 1989)

Dr. Seuss's ABC, by Theodore Geisel. (Random House, 1963)

Easy as Pie, by Marcia Folsom and Michael Folsom. (Houghton Mifflin, 1986)

Eating the Alphabet, by Lois Ehlert. (Harcourt, 1989)

It Begins with an A, by S. Calmenson. (Hyperion, 1993)

My Picture Dictionary, by Diane Snowball and Robyn Green. (Mondo, 1994)

On Market Street, by Arnold Lobel. (Greenwillow, 1988)

Tomorrow's Alphabet, by George Shannon. (William Morrow, 1996)

Make a Class Alphabet Book

Once you and the children have read several alphabet books, you might want to make a 26-page alphabet book centered around things in your classroom. Have children illustrate each letter on a different page or take photos and print a simple caption on the bottom of each page. Some teachers just label each picture with a one-word name. Others print the word and then a short sentence. Look around the room and see what you have for each letter. You may have to "plant" a few things or pictures of things you would not normally have in your classroom so they can be found when it is time to make that page. Classrooms are all different but here are some likely possibilities (with a few objects "planted" for obstinate letters like Q and X):

A alphabet or arms

B boys or boxes

C computer or couch

D desks or doors

E easel or ears

F flag or feet

G girls or glue

H hands or hamster

I ivy or intercom

J jackets or jars

K keys or kangaroo (stuffed)

L lunchboxes or legs

M magazines or markers

N numbers or noses

O overhead or orange things

P pencils or paper

Q quilt or queen

R rug or rabbit or red things

S sink or scissors

T teacher or tape

U umbrellas or uniforms

V vase or violets

W windows or walls

X xylophone or x-ray

Y yardstick or yellow things

Z zippers or zebras

ASSESSING PROGRESS

Assessment is an ongoing process for experienced teachers who have become good kid watchers. As the children respond to the various activities, teachers notice who can do what. Write down what you notice and you have anecdotal records! Samples—particularly writing samples and audiotaped samples of children reading—are also informative. By comparing samples obtained over a period of time, growth can be determined and validated. Here are some of the concepts and strategies you can assess during the first 4-6 weeks of first grade and some guidelines for making these assessments.

Print Concepts

Print is what you read and write. Print includes all the funny little marks—letters, punctuation, space between words and paragraphs—which translate into familiar spoken language. In English, we read across the page in a left-to-right fashion. Because our eyes can only see a few words during each stop (called a *fixation*), we must actually move our eyes several times to read one line of print. (These movements occur so rapidly, sophisticated readers aren't even aware of them, and we feel like we can see many more words at once. This, however, is an optical illusion!) When we finish a line, we make a return sweep and start all over again. If there are sentences at the top of a page and a picture in the middle and more sentences at the bottom, we read the top first and then the bottom. We start at the front of a book and go towards the back.

In addition to learning how to move our eyes to follow the print, beginners must also learn the *jargon* of print. Jargon refers to all the words we use to talk about reading and writing and includes terms such as *letter*, *sound*, *word*, and *sentence*. We use this jargon constantly as we try to teach children how to read:

"Look at the **first word** in the **second sentence.** How does that **word begin?** What **letter** makes that **sound?"**

Using some jargon is essential to talking with children about reading and writing, but children who have had limited exposure to the written word are often hopelessly confused by this jargon. Although all children speak in words, they don't know words exist as separate entities until they are put in the presence of reading and writing. **To many children, *letters* are what you get in the mailbox, *sounds* are horns and bells and doors slamming, and *sentences* are what you serve if you get caught committing a crime!** These children are unable to follow our "simple" instructions because we are using words for which they have no meaning or an entirely different meaning.

Many children come to first grade understanding this jargon and already able to track print. From being read to in the lap position, they have noticed how the eyes "jump" across the lines of print as someone is reading. They have watched people write grocery lists or thank-you notes to Grandma and have observed the top-bottom, left-right movement. Often, they have typed on a computer and observed these print conventions. Because they have had someone to talk with them about reading and writing, they have learned much of the jargon. While writing down a dictated thank-you note to Grandma, Dad may say,

> "Say your **sentence** one **word** at a time if you want me to write it. I can't write as fast as you can talk."

When a child named Brad notices that **birthday** starts with the same letter as his name, he may be told,

> "Yes, **Brad** and **birthday** both start with the **letter b** and when you say **Brad** and **birthday**, you can hear the **sound** the **b** makes."

Applying a Print Checklist

From their reading and writing encounters, many entering first graders have learned how to track print and what we are talking about when we ask them to look at the **first word** or the **last letter** or the fact that **Robert** and **Rasheed** begin with the **same sound**. These print concepts are essential to beginning a successful journey toward literacy and thus are some of the most important concepts to assess during the first month of school.

Many teachers use a checklist such as the following:

Concepts of Print Checklist	Aug.	Sept.
• Starts on left		
• Reads/writes left-to-right		
• Makes return sweep to next line		
• Matches words by pointing to each word as reading		
• Can point to just one word		
• Can point to the first word and the last word		
• Can point to just one letter		
• Can point to the first letter and the last letter		

Teachers can use the checklist as children are reading big books or during the daily chart reading time. As different children volunteer to read, asks them to point to what they are reading. Also ask them if they can point to just one word, point to the first and last words, point to just one letter, and point to the first and last letters of a word. If they are successful, put a plus in the column showing what they have demonstrated. When each child has a plus for two different days (two plusses in total), the teacher assumes this child has the concept and doesn't check this anymore for this child. When a child demonstrates that he has all these concepts, the teacher draws a line through his name and focuses the instruction and assessment on children who have not yet demonstrated these concepts.

Many teachers work individually or in small groups with children who still have not mastered these concepts by rereading big books or charts and focusing children on these concepts. This combination of daily reading of predictable text with emphasis on print concepts done first with the whole class and then with a small group or individuals who need more help will usually result in all children having learned these critical print concepts by October. **A few children may need continued individual attention as October activities begin. Knowing who these children are and what they need will allow you to give them little snatches of instruction as they engage in reading and writing along with everyone else.**

Phonemic Awareness

As discussed under the section on rhyming, *phonemic awareness* is the ability to manipulate words. It includes knowing that the sentence:

I had a bad day at school today.

has more words than the sentence:

I got mad.

It includes being able to clap syllables in words and knowing that the word **motorcycles** takes more claps than the word **car**. Perhaps the most critical phonemic awareness ability to assess towards the end of the first month of first grade is the ability to come up with a word that rhymes with another word.

Children who have phonemic awareness can tell you that **bike** rhymes with **Mike** and that **book** does not. After students have participated in the activities suggested for *There's a Wocket in My Pocket*, they can make up silly rhymes for objects in the classroom. They can get The Hungry Thing to eat their food by making up a word that rhymes with what they want to feed it.

You can assess children's phonemic awareness by observing their ability to do these rhyming word tasks as you do the activities with the whole class. Just as for print concepts, a child needs two plusses on two different days before deciding that the child had developed the concept. Work individually or in a small group with children who after 3-4 weeks of class activities have not caught on. As you move into October, most children have the desired level of phonemic awareness, and you know which children needed continued nudges toward developing this awareness as you move into more advanced decoding and spelling activities.

Word Learning

If you sit down with first graders on the first day of school and try to determine if they can read by giving them a simple book to read or testing them on some common words such as **the, and, of,** or **with**, you would probably conclude that most first graders can't read yet. But many first graders can read and write some words. Most children who have had reading and writing experiences have learned some words. The words they learn are usually concrete words that are "important to them." **A child who knows 10-15 words may not be able to read much, but he has accomplished a critical task; he has learned how to learn words.**

All children should have learned some words during the early first-grade activities. To assess their word learning, you may want to check their ability to read the names of the children in the class and some of the most interesting words such as **fox**, **hen**, and **pig** from a big book such as *Hattie and the Fox*. For children who came to school already knowing some concrete words, you may want to see if they have learned some of the high-frequency words —such as **like**, **is**, **in**, **the**— often repeated in big books and in many of the chart articles.

The expectation should not be that anyone is learning *all* words (although children who came to school already reading will astound you with how little repetition they need to learn a word!), but everyone is adding *some* words to the store of words they can read.

Letter Names and Sounds

Finally, many children have learned some letter names and sounds. They can't usually recognize all 26 letters in both upper- and lower case, and they often don't know the sounds of **w** or **c**, but they have learned the names and sounds for the most-common letters. Usually, the letter names and sounds children know are based on those concrete words they can read and write.

We assess each child's knowledge of letter names and sounds by showing him a sheet containing all the letters in upper- and lower-case form and asking him to point to any letters he knows. The letters he knows can be

noted on his record sheet with an *n* for *name*. Once he has indicated the letters he knows, we point to some of the letters he didn't name and ask:

> "Can you tell me what sound this letter makes?"

If he gives an appropriate sound, we indicate this with an *s* for *sound* on his record sheet.

Next, we point to some of the letters he hasn't identified and ask:

> "Do you know any words that begin with this letter?"

We indicate with a *w* for *word* any letters he didn't give us names or sounds for but for which he has a word association.

As we move into October, the decoding and spelling focus of the next month will be on student learning of high-frequency words which occur over and over in reading and writing. Learning these words enables students to develop some independent reading skills and to learn how letters and sounds go together to make words. **The chapter will continue to include activities with opportunities for children to learn print concepts, develop phonemic awareness, learn concrete words, and start associating letter names and sounds with words.** By assessing these four critical concepts, we know which children have not moved as far along in these understandings and we can continue to instruct, monitor, and assess their progress.

OCTOBER

In October of first grade, most classrooms have started moving into some teacher-guided reading in basal readers or other books which are early first-grade level. Daily class routines should also include writing time (in which children write about whatever they want and then share what they have written with the group), teacher read-aloud time, and independent-reading time (during which each child "reads" a self-selected book by himself or with a friend). The independent reading many first graders do early in the year is the pretend reading of familiar stories or the reading of the pictures in informational picture books with topics such as animals or trucks.

Shared/Guided Reading, Self-Selected Reading, and Writing are three components of a good, balanced literacy program. As such, they should occupy the majority of the instructional time in any first-grade classroom. The fourth component, Working with Words—learning to read and spell high-frequency words and to decode and spell lots of less-frequent words—is the focus of this and the following chapters.

The activities in this and other chapters help children develop their word skills. These word skills are worthless, however, if children are not doing lots of reading and writing. In fact, *only* if there are lots of opportunities to apply their word skills in reading and writing will children get enough practice with words to become truly automatic and fluent in dealing with words. Remember that the activities described here are only part of a balanced first-grade literacy program.

By the end of October, you will have introduced the following:

- A Word Wall on which is displayed many high-frequency words
- Use of the Word Wall as a visual cue for spelling these high-frequency words
- The strategy of using children's own names to learn more about letters and sounds

- Tongue Twisters as a way to learn and review beginning consonant sounds
- The ability to cross-check, using context and phonics clues(in Guess the Covered Word activities)

Additional Resources

Here are a few resources with rich descriptions of the three core components—shared/guided reading, teacher read-aloud/self-selected reading, and writing:

And with a Light Touch: Learning about Reading, Writing and Teaching with First Graders, by Carol Avery (Heinemann, 1993)

Invitations, by Regie Routman (Heinemann, 1994)

Classrooms that Work: They can All Read and Write, by Patricia M. Cunningham and Richard L. Allington (HarperCollins, 1994)

The Four Blocks: A Framework for Reading and Writing in Classrooms that Work, by Pat Cunningham and Dottie Hall (1995) [This video is available from I.E.S.S. by calling 800-644-5280]

WORKING WITH WORDS BLOCK

30 min.

Remember that the Working with Words Block is only one part of a balanced literacy program, and **30 to 35 minutes is an appropriate amount of time for most first-grade classrooms to spend each day on word activities.**

The first 10 minutes should be spent practicing the high-frequency words on the Word Wall. The Word Wall section beginning on the next page presents some basics about creating a Word Wall.

That then leaves 20-25 minutes for an activity in which students learn to decode and spell words that follow patterns. During the remaining 20-25 minutes of time allotted for word activities, a different activity could be done on different days. Three such activities are described on the following pages: Connecting Children's Names to Letters and Sounds, Tongue Twisters, and Guess the Covered Word.

WORD WALL

A Word Wall is a wall on which to display words—but not just any words—truly important words. Most teachers reserve a bulletin board or use the space above their chalkboard for these important words. Many teachers begin their Word Wall by adding the name of the special child chosen each day during August and September. (If you tell children that the Word Wall is where you put really important words, they will believe you when they see their names there because first graders know they are really important people!) Regardless of whether or not you start your Word Wall with the names of your students, the other really important words for first graders are the words that make up every other word they read and write (see page 30). Recognizing these high-frequency words helps children to read; being able to spell high frequency words will help children to write.

Adding Words

Add five new words to the wall each week. **The best words to use are those that occur frequently in whatever the children are reading.** If you made a Special Child chart for each student in August/September, you can select high-frequency words from those charts. Thus, the first five words might be:

    boy   girl   is   has   like

Write the words on sheets of colored paper. (It doesn't matter what colors, but avoid dark colors on which letters don't show up!) The words need to be large enough ($2^1/2$" to 3") to be seen from anywhere in the room. If two or more words begin with the same letter, use a different color of paper for each of those words. After writing each word with a thick, black permanent marker, cut around the outline of the letters to emphasize handwriting features and to make the words more visually interesting. Put the words on the chalkboard as you review them with students. Display some of the charts that have sentences containing the words, and help students locate the words on the charts.

Once you have reviewed the words with the students, you can put each word on the Word Wall next to the letter that begins the word.

Here is a partial sample of what your Word Wall might look like.

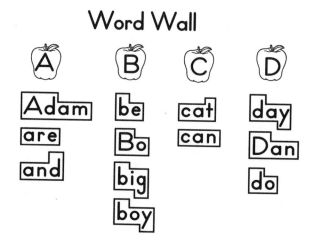

Daily Word Practice

1. Begin by giving each child a half sheet of handwriting paper numbered 1-5.
2. Call out the first word on the wall and have children glue their eyes to the written word (**visual**).
3. After you have read the word, have the children cheer for the word—"B-O-Y—boy!" (**auditory rhythmic**).
4. Have each child write the word on the first line of his paper (**kinesthetic**). Write the word on the board or overhead projector as children write it on their papers to emphasize the correct formation of the letters.
5. Repeat the procedure for the four remaining words.
6. After all five words are looked at, cheered for, and written, lead the children to check the spelling and handwriting by drawing around the shapes of the words.

The first week, call out the same five words every day and have children practice looking at, cheering for, and writing the words. Next week, add five more words. If you are still using high-frequency words from the student charts, you might add:

> **he   she   can   play   to**

Each day when new words are added, follow the same procedure. Locate those words in the context in which children have read them (chart, big book, basal, or other book). Call out five words for children to look at, cheer for, write and check. Most teachers add the five new words on Monday and call out the new words on Monday and Tuesday. Wednesday, Thursday, and Friday can then be used to call out some of the words added in previous weeks so that there is constant review and practice for all the words on the wall.

This procedure of adding five new words a week, practicing those words for a few days, and then spending the remaining days of the week practicing words from previous weeks continues until there are approximately 110 words (not counting children's names) **on the wall.** Try to add the last word to the Word Wall by April 15th (pay your taxes and put the last word on the wall!) and then do lots of reviewing and practice with these words until school is out. **These words are so important that we want to assure some "overlearning" so that most children will still be able to read and spell them after a long summer away from school.**

Word Selection

Use the list on the next page when choosing words to put on the Word Wall, and then decide the sequence of their introduction on the Word Wall. The list of 110 high-utility first grade wall words includes:

- The most frequent words needed to read and write

- At least one example for the most common sound for each initial consonant (b, c, d, f, g, h, j, k, l, m, n, p, r, s, t, v, w, x, y, z)

- At least one example for the sound for ch, sh, th, wh, and qu

- An example for spelling patterns from which many rhyming words can be spelled. (Boldfaced words have helpful spelling patterns that can be transferred to additional words for reading and writing.)

110 High-Frequency First Grade Words

after	**down**	I	**out**	they
all	**eat**	**in**	over	**thing**
am	favorite	is	people	this
and	for	**it**	**play**	to
animal	friend	**jump**	pretty	up
are	from	**kick**	**quit**	us
at	**fun**	**like**	**rain**	very
be	get	little	**ride**	want
because	girl	**look**	said	was
best	give	**made**	**saw**	we
big	go	**make**	school	**went**
boy	good	me	**see**	what
brother	**had**	**my**	she	**when**
but	has	**new**	sister	where
can	have	**nice**	some	who
can't	he	**night**	**talk**	**why**
car	her	no	teacher	**will**
children	here	**not**	**tell**	with
come	**him**	of	**that**	won't
day	his	off	the	you
did	house	**old**	them	your
do	**how**	on	there	zoo

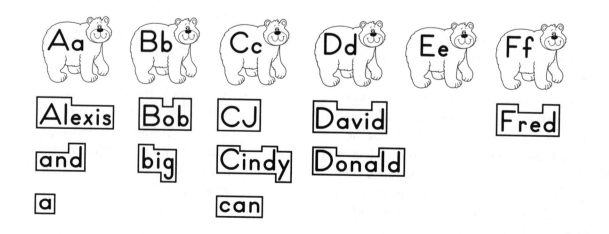

CONNECTING CHILDREN'S NAMES TO LETTERS AND SOUNDS

20 min.

Let's begin the lesson with some important information about learning and memory. **There are two kinds of learning, and your brain has two memory stores. Things we just "do over and over" until we learn them are put in our rote memory store. This area has limited capacity, and if something that has been put there is not practiced in a while, the space is given to something more current.** ("What was her phone number? Before she went to Florida, I called her every day and knew it, but now I will have to look it up again!") **The other memory store, the associative store, has unlimited capacity and we can find things in there we haven't thought about for years if the memory is triggered by something such as an image, smell, or sound.**

Storing Information in the Associative Memory Store

The trick to putting something in the associative store rather than in the rote store is to create an *association*. A child who is trying to remember that a particular shape turned a particular way is called "d" and that it has the

sound we hear in **doughnut** and **dog** cannot associate the name and the sound of **d** with **doughnut** and **dog** unless she can read the words **doughnut** and **dog**. The child must just try to remember that the letter is called **d** and it has the sound heard in **doughnut** and **dog**. The child must put all this information in her rote-memory stores and if she doesn't use it for awhile (as when she is on winter vacation for two weeks!), the space in her rote memory will be used up by something else, and she will have to learn it all over again!

Making Associations with Names

The only way to help children put names and sound knowledge of letters in their associative stores rather than their rote stores is to make sure they can read some words which contain the letters. If you did the August/September activities that used student names, you can now use the names as associative links to letter names and sounds.

Some letter-sound associations were emphasized as student names were introduced. Now that all the names are displayed, however, and most children have learned most of the names, we can begin to solidify some of that knowledge of letter names and sounds. Imagine that the names of our children displayed on the Word Wall or name board are:

Adam	Delano	Octavius
Amber T.	Erica	Rasheed
Amber M.	Erin	Robert
Bianca	Joseph	Sam
Bo	Julio	Shawonda
Brittany	Kelsie	Sheila
Catherine	Kevin	Tara
Cindy	Matt	
David	Mike	

Steps for Making Associations with Names

1. Begin the activity by giving each child a sentence strip with his name on it.

2. Choose a letter that many children have in their names and that usually has its expected sound. With this class you might choose the letter **r**.

3. Have each child whose name has an **r** in it come to the front of the class holding his name card.

4. Count all the **r**'s. (There are ten **r**'s in all.)

5. Have the children with names containing an **r** divide themselves into those whose names **begin** with an **R**—Robert and Rasheed; those whose names **end** with **r**— Amber T. and Amber M.; and those with an **r** that is **neither the first nor the last letter**—Brittany, Erica, Tara, Erin, and Catherine.

6. Finally, say each name slowly, stretching out the letters, and decide if you can hear the usual sound of the selected letter. In the case of the letter **r**, it can be heard in each name.

Choose another letter and let all the children with names containing the new letter come to the front of the class and display their name cards. Count the number of times the letter occurs and then have the children divide themselves into groups according to whether their names have the selected letter as the first letter, the last letter, or neither the first nor the last letter. Finally, say the names stretching them out and decide if you can hear the usual sound that letter makes. **D** would be a good second choice. You would have **David** and **Delano** beginning with **D**; **David** and **Rasheed** ending with **d**; and **Cindy**, **Shawonda** and **Adam** with **d**'s that are neither the first nor the last letters. (Point out that **David** has more than one **d**. As you say the **David**, allow him to choose which group to join.) Again, the usual sound of **d** is heard in all the names.

Continue choosing letters and having children come to the front of the room with their name cards until you have sorted for several different letters represented by the names. When doing the letters **s**, **c**, **t**, and **j**, be sure to point out that they can have two sounds and that the **th** in **Catherine** and the **sh** in **Sheila**, **Shawonda**, and **Rasheed** have their own special sounds. You probably wouldn't sort out the names with an **h** because although the names **Shawanda**, **Sheila**, **Rasheed**, **Catherine** and **Joseph** have **h**'s, the **h** sound is not represented by any of these. The same would go for the **p**, which only occurs in **Joseph**. **When you have the children come down for the vowels *a*, *e*, *i*, *o* and *u*, count and then sort the children according to first, last, and neither first nor last, but do not try to listen for the sounds. Explain that vowels have lots of different sounds and that they will learn more about the vowels and their sounds later in the year.**

TONGUE TWISTERS

15 min.

Tongue twisters are wonderful for review of consonants because they give lots of word examples for particular sounds and are such fun to say. Do one or two each day. First, just say them and have the students repeat them after you (*not* while you are saying them). Have students say them as fast as they can and as slowly as they can.

Write the tongue twisters on a chart or poster and call attention to the first letter of each word. Have students read the tongue twisters several times. You may want to have students illustrate the tongue twisters.

Add one or two Tongue Twisters each day—always introducing them verbally first. After you write the new ones, review some of the old ones. Leave the charts or posters displayed and refer students to them if they forget or become confused about a sound.

Here are some Tongue Twisters to get you started. You can create different ones, but be sure to use children's names from your class when they have the right letters and sounds!

Billy's baby brother bopped Betty.

Carol can catch caterpillars.

Dottie dawdled during dinner.

Frank's father fried five fish.

Gorgeous Gail gets good grades.

Hungry Hannah happily had hot dogs.

Jack juggled Jill's jewelry.

Kevin's kitten kissed Karen.

Laurie loves licking lemon lollipops.

My mother makes marvelous macaroni.

Naughty Ned needed nails and nickels.

Peter Piper picked a peck of pickled peppers.

Rapid Roger runs races.

Sam's sister slurps soup.

Tom took ten turtles to town.

Vic visited very vicious vultures.

William went west with Willy Winston.

Yoland yelled, "You yanked my yellow yo-yo!"

Zeke's zany zebra had a zipper.

Additional Tongue Twisters

Here are some wonderful Tongue Twister books:

Alphabet Annie Announces an All-American Album, by Susan Purviance and Marcia O'Shell. (Houghton Mifflin, 1988)

Animalia, by Graeme Base. (Abrams, 1987)

The Biggest Tongue Twister Book in the World, by Gyles Brandeth. (Sterling, 1978)

Busy Buzzing Bumblebees and other Tongue Twisters, by Alvin Schwartz. (HarperCollins, 1992)

Six Sick Sheep, by Jan Cole. (Morrow, 1993)

A Twister of Twists, A Tangler of Tongues, by Alvin Schwartz. (HarperCollins, 1972)

GUESS THE COVERED WORD

15 min.

Learning to Cross-Check

The ability to use the consonants in a word along with the context is an important decoding strategy. **Children must learn to do two things simultaneously—think about what would make sense and think about letters and sounds.** Most children would prefer to do one or the other, but not both. Thus, some children guess something that is sensible but ignore the letter sounds they know. Other children guess something which is close to the sounds but makes no sense in the sentence!

In order to help children cross-check meaning with sound, do the following:

- First, have children guess a missing word that has no letters revealed. There are generally many possibilities for a word that will fit the context.

- Next, reveal some letters to narrow the number of possibilities.

- Finally, show all the letters and help children confirm the word that makes sense and matches the letters.

For each cross-checking lesson, you will need to write sentences on the board or chart and cover the word to be guessed with two sticky notes. The first sticky note should cover the first letters of the word up to the first vowel. (For the first lessons, each word will only have a single consonant before the first vowel. A more-advanced version of the activity can include words with letter combinations such as **sh**, **br**, and so on.) The second sticky note will cover the first vowel and all the other letters in the word. When covering the words, tear or cut your sticky notes so that each is exactly as wide as the letter or letters it covers. By doing so, you will provide students with the additional clue of word length. **Word length, beginning letters, and common sense are all powerful clues to the identity of an unknown word.**

Here are some sample sentences. (The bold word in each sentence will be the covered word that students will try to guess.) Remember that using your children's names helps to keep them engaged!

Carl likes to eat **cookies**.

Paula likes to eat **macaroni**.

Miguel likes to eat **hamburgers**.

Nick likes to eat **pizza**.

Show the children the sentences and explain that they will read each sentence and guess the covered word. Allow students to try to guess the covered word of the first sentence. Use a space on your chalkboard or chart next to the sentence to record each guess that makes sense. If a guess does not make sense, explain why but do not write this guess.

When you have written several guesses, remove the paper which covers the first letter. Draw a line through each guess which does not begin with this letter and ask if there are any more guesses which make sense and start with the letter. If there are more guesses, write these. Be sure all guesses both make sense and start correctly. Some children will begin guessing anything that begins with **c**. Respond with something like, "**Cars** does begin with a **c**, but I can't write **cars** because people don't eat **cars**."

When you have written all guesses which make sense and begin correctly, uncover the word. Let the children see if the word is one they guessed. If the correct guess had been made, praise the students' efforts. If not, say, "That was a tough one!" and go on to the next sentence. Continue with each sentence going through the same steps:

1. Read the sentence and write three or four guesses which make sense.

2. Uncover the letter (up to the vowel). Draw a line through any guesses which don't begin with the correct letter.

3. Have students make more guesses which both make sense *and* begin with the correct letter. Write the guesses.

4. Uncover the whole word and see if any of the students' guesses were correct.

Carl likes to eat c[____]. ~~apples~~
candy
~~salad~~
cupcakes
corn

Paula likes to eat [____].

ASSESSING PROGRESS

As mentioned in the August/September chapter, assessment is an ongoing process and children at different stages of literacy development should be assessed on different abilities. At this point, you should know which children are still having difficulty with any of the critical concepts described in the August/September section. Use the assessment suggestions (on pages 22-25) to determine if any those children having difficulty with print concepts , phonemic awareness, word learning, or letter name and sound knowledge have made progress in October.

Remember that some children take much more practice and repetition than others before they understand these critical but complex concepts. You will probably have some children who have not yet mastered some of these concepts, but they should demonstrate some growth over this month's literacy activities.

Assisting Children Having Difficulty

Make a list of children who still need continued guidance with print concepts, phonemic awareness, word learning, or letter name and sound knowledge. Keep this list in a place you look at regularly and you will remember to give the extra little bit of individual support that makes a big difference. **Here are some possible "nudges" for those who still need help.**

Print Concepts
For those children who lack print concepts, have them come up and point to words with you as the rest of the class rereads a page from a big book or a chart. Help them to identify the first word, the last word, to find two words that begin with the same letter, etc. As you are writing a morning message or some other shared writing activity, ask them to come show you where to start and where to put the next word when you have finished one line.

Phonemic Awareness
For those children who lack phonemic awareness, be sure that they are saying rhymes, tongue twisters, etc., with you and the rest of the class, not just listening while others say them. These children might come up and lead the class in repeating favorite chants, etc. After someone else has identified the rhyming words, or words that begin alike. Have the child repeat what that child said. "Bo, can you tell me what words Rasheed said rhymed?"

Word Learning

Perhaps some children cannot yet read the words you have added to the wall, but they should be able to locate and identify them. As you are calling out Word Wall words for the daily practice, ask children who are slow at learning these words to go up and point to the words. You might be calling out **me**. You could say, "I want a word under the letter **m**. It is the pink word, **me**. Bobby can you go up and point to the pink word **me** so that we are all looking at the right word?" If children cannot yet read the word but they can locate it on the wall, they will be able to find when writing and that will provide the extra practice needed for them to be able to eventually read the word.

Letter Names and Sounds

Some children need a lot of practice to learn letter names and sounds. If you have children who still cannot name a lot of the letters, begin each Making Words lesson, described in the November section by having the children hold up and name the letters. Call on the children you are worrying about to name each letter after you have named it and while they are holding it up. "Everyone hold up your **s**. Good Bobby, you are holding up the right letter. What is this letter's name?" Daily practice with the letters—particularly when they are tangible letters you can hold and move around to make words will usually result in even the most hard-to-teach child learning the names and sounds for most of the letters.

In November, continue to immerse students with the Working with Words activities begun in October (as well as the other Reading and Writing activities which are on-going in your classroom). This chapter will outline two new activities to add to your Working with Words repetoire: On-the-Back activities and Making Words activities.

Continue to add five new words to the Word Wall each week, but now children can use the backs of their Word Wall papers for On-the-Back activities. Making Words is another new activity that is an active, multi-level, multi-sensory activity that helps children learn how to look for patterns in words. Continue to use Tongue Twisters to review beginning consonant sounds. Use Guess the Covered Word to practice cross-checking, plus children see how changing just one letter or its location in the word can change the entire word!

By the end of November, you will have introduced the following:

- On-the-Back activities that help transfer Word Wall words to lots of other words used during reading and writing.
- Making Words—a three-step, multi-level, multi-sensory, hands-on activity.
  Step 1—Making the Words to develop phonemic awareness and to figure out how words work.
  Step 2—Sorting the Words to help the brain become a pattern detector for beginning sounds, rhyming words, and endings
  Step 3—Transferring the Words to extend the patterns to other words students will read and write

WORD WALL

10 min.

ON-THE-BACK ACTIVITY

10 min.

As outlined in the October chapter, continue to add five new Word Wall words each week, usually choosing the words from high-frequency words children have read in books during Shared/Guided Reading. Continue calling out the five words each day, having children cheer for the words and then write them. As they write them, write them along with the children and model the correct handwriting.

Again, remember that the Working with Words activities should take up only 30-35 minutes of the day. The first ten minutes of these word-related activities will be taken up by the daily Word Wall activity. You may then use the remaining 20-25 minutes for one of several different activities: On-the-Back activities, Making Words activities, Guess the Covered Word, or Tongue Twisters.

The On-the-Back activity is so named because students do the activity on the backs of the handwriting papers used for the Word Wall activity. On-the-Back activities are designed to help children learn that some of the words on the Word Wall can help them spell lots of other words. You might present the activity by saying something like the following. (For this example, assume that the word **it** is already on the Word Wall.)

"All of the words on the Word Wall are important words because we see them again and again in books and because knowing them helps us write. Some words are also important because they help spell lots of other words that rhyme with them.

"**It** is one of those helpful words. Today, we are going to practice using **it** to spell five other words. Circle the word **it** on this week's list of new words.

"Turn your paper over and number the lines from 1 to 5.

"What if you were writing about how a dog bit your brother. The word **it** will help you spell **bit**. Say **bit** slowly and listen for the first sound. Yes, **bit** begins with the letter **b**. Everyone write **b**. Say the words **it** and **bit** and listen to the way they rhyme. Write **it** after **b** and you can spell **bit**."

The On-the-Back lesson continues with four more possible scenarios in which students would need to use **it** to help them spell words that rhyme with **it**:

"What if you were writing about a baseball game and wanted to say you hit the ball? Say **hit** slowly. Write the first letter, **h**, and then finish the word with the spelling pattern **it**.

"You might be writing about how you taught your dog to sit." (Everyone writes **s-i-t**.)

"You might write about going to the mall to buy a new winter jacket because last year's jacket wouldn't fit." (Everyone writes **f** and then **it**.)

The final step of the activity should involve a more-challenging word and could be presented like this:

"The fifth rhyming word is one that begins with **two** letters. What if you're writing about your cat and want to tell that when she is really mad, she will spit at something? Say **spit** slowly with me, stretching it out and listening for two sounds at the beginning. Good, you hear an **s** and a **p**. Now write the **s** and the **p** and then finish the word with the spelling pattern **it**."

When you present the On-the-Back rhyming activity, put it in a "What if you are writing and need to spell...?" context, because knowing how rhyming words help you spell other words is only useful if you do it when you are writing and trying to spell a particular word. Use several examples and choose words that students might actually need to write. Most lessons should include some words with single beginning letters and others where you have to listen for two letters. Model how you "stretch out the word" to listen for the beginning sound and then finish the word with the spelling pattern—the vowel and what follows. Many teachers attach a star, sticker, or some other visible symbols to the Word Wall words that are helpful in spelling other words. This way, children will be in the habit of thinking of these words as they are trying to spell a new word.

Here are a few more On-the-Back activity words that can be learned from existing Word Wall words. The first bold word is a word most teachers have on their Word Walls by the end of November.

At will help students spell **cat, bat, hat, brat**, and **flat**.

Am will help students spell **ham, Sam, Pam, clam**, and **Spam**.

And will help students spell **hand, sand, band, stand**, and **brand**.

Can will help students spell **Dan, man, ran, tan**, and **plan**.

Will will help students spell **Bill, fill, pill, still**, and **spill**.

MAKING WORDS

20 min.

Making Words is an exciting, high-energy activity. In this activity children arrange letters to make words. Students begin by making little words using a few of the letters and then progress to bigger words. The final word includes all the letters, and children are eager to discover the word that can be made from *all* the letters. Making Words is an activity in which children learn how to look for patterns in words and how changing just one letter or its location in the word changes the whole word. The little bit of extra preparation needed for the lesson will yield *big* results as children delight in their ability to create and manipulate words!

Making Cards and Holders

The letter cards used in this activity can be easily made with tagboard or index cards, black and red markers, and scissors. Make a set for each child and one for yourself. To make each letter card, cut a square from the tagboard or index card. Students' squares should be about 1½" in size, and your cards should be larger to be displayed in a pocket chart. Print a lowercase letter in the center of each card in black. Turn the card over and print the letter in uppercase. Vowels can be set apart from consonants by printing them in red.

Student word holders can be made by cutting file folders into 2" x 12" strips. For each holder, fold up about ¼" of a long side and tape the edges to make a pocket. The letter cards can be tucked into the shallow fold to make words in the holder.

For most Making Words lessons, you will give each student 5-8 letters (including two vowels) to make 10-15 words. For the first lessons, however, limit the number of letters to five and include only one vowel. The five letters will make 8-10 words. The following pages present an example of a first Making Words lesson as it is first *prepared* by the you and then *taught* in a first-grade classroom.

Preparing the Lesson

The five letters that will be used for the lesson are **a**, **d**, **h**, **n**, and **s**, and **hands** is the word that will end the lesson. Pull out the letter cards marked with the letters **h**, **a**, **n**, **d**, and **s**. Then, brainstorm lots of little words that can be made from the letters in **hands**.

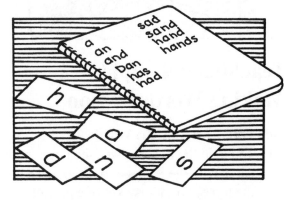

Decide which of the many words that you have brainstormed will make an easy and successful first lesson. Write these words on large index cards. (If the letters only make 8-10 words, use them all!)

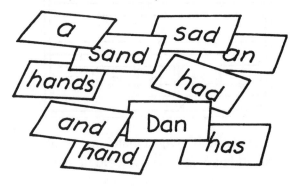

The letter and word cards are put in a large envelope. On the outside of the envelope, the teacher writes the words in the order the children are to make them and then writes the patterns to be sorted for. Several lessons can be prepared at one time and the envelopes can be filed in a cardboard box. (As additional lessons are prepared, they too can be added to the box.) When it is time to present a **Making Words** lesson to the class, the teacher simply selects an envelope from the box.

Teaching a Sample Making Words Lesson

Step One—Making the Words

1. To begin the lesson, place the large index cards with the letters **a**, **d**, **h**, **n**, and **s** in the top or bottom pocket of a pocket chart at the front of the classroom.

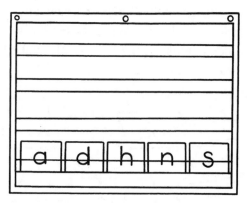

Each child is given a matching set of small letter cards and a word holder.

2. Hold up and name the letter on each large card in the pocket chart. The children hold up and name their matching cards.

For these first lessons, you and children will show both the upper- and lowercase letters and discuss that the one red letter is the vowel. Children count the letters and determine that they have four black letters (the consonants) and one red letter (the vowel) for a total of five.

3. The children get ready to make words by placing their letters in a row in front of their holders.

4. Tell the children that every word must have a vowel. Today each child has only one vowel—the red **a**. The **a** can be put in the word holder, and the child can work around it since every word will need it.

Write a **2** on the board and say, "The first word I want you to make has just two letters—your **a** plus one more. Everyone say **an**. I brought **an** apple to eat at snack time. Find a letter to add to the **a** to spell **an**."

Have the children say **an**—stretching out the end of **an**. Watch as many children put the card with the letter **n** in the holder after the **a**. Then, let one child who has made **an** correctly make **an** with the large letters in the pocket chart.

Say, "Good, **a-n** spells **an**. Everyone make **an** in your holder, and we are ready to make another word."

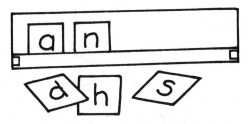

After the word is made with the large letters, the index card with the word **an** is placed in the pocket chart. The index card words will be sorted for patterns after all the words are made.

5. Next, write a **3** on the board. Tell the children, "Leave the word **an** in your holder and add just one letter to make the word **and**. Carolyn **and** Bo had birthdays last week. Everyone say **and**. Stretch out the end of **and** and try to hear the letter that makes the sound at the end. Put that letter in your holder after the **an**."

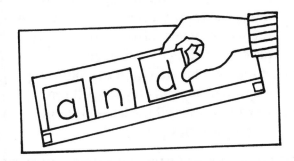

As children attempt to make the word, choose a child who has made the word correctly and have the child make the word in the pocket chart using the large letters. Place the index card with the word **and** on it in the pocket chart. Then confirm that each child has correctly spelled the word using his own letters before moving to the next word.

An important way to keep the lesson moving is to avoid waiting for everyone to make the word before it is made in the pocket chart with the big letters. Once the word has been made in the pocket chart, however, everyone should have it made before the lesson progresses to a new word. Some children look at the word in the pocket chart and copy it.

6. Tell the class that the same three letters that spell **and** will spell the name **Dan** if they are put in a different order and if the first letter card is turned over to show the capital-letter side. The class says the word **Dan**, stretching out the letters and listening to the order of the sounds. (Some teachers call this an "abracadabra" word because it is "magic" and can be changed.)

It is very important to have children actually say each word that they will be spelling. They need to hear themselves making the sounds if they are going to transfer this ability to spelling words as they write.

Find someone with the word **Dan** spelled correctly (and with a capital **D**) and have the child make the word in the pocket chart using the large letters. Then put the index card with the word **Dan** in the pocket chart and have each child confirm or correct his letters.

7. You and the children should continue to make three-letter words. Say, "Take all the letters but your vowel **a** out of your holder. The next word we will spell is **has**. Carlos **has** brown eyes. Everyone say **has**. Stretch out the sounds to hear where the letters go."

As with previous words, do not wait for everyone to spell the word correctly before choosing someone to spell it in the pocket chart. Then place the index card with the word **has** in the pocket chart and make sure each child has spelled it correctly before the lesson proceeds to a new word.

8. Have students make new words by changing letters. Say, "This time, we are going to change the end of the word. Leave the letters **h** and **a** in your letter holder, but take away the letter **s**. Add another letter and you can spell **had**. Everyone say **had**. We **had** a rainy weekend."

"The next word is **sad**. Change the first letter to turn **had** into **sad**. Everyone say **sad**. What do you hear at the beginning of **sad**?"

9. Erase the **3** from the board and write a **4**.

"Now we are going to make a four-letter word. If you add a letter somewhere, you can change **sad** into **sand**. Everyone say **sand** slowly with me. Try to hear where you can add a letter to make **sad** into **sand**."

Next, tell the students to change just the first letter of **sand** and they will have the word **hand**.

Making the words in this step may be difficult for most children, but remember this is a multilevel lesson. It started out very easy and you insured success for struggling students by having them make each word after it was made with the pocket-chart letters, but now you need something to challenge star students. This step (and the following step when students try to spell the word that uses all the letters) should accomplish this goal!

10. Before the final word is made, tell the children that when you plan a **Making Words** lesson you always have a "secret" word that can be made with all the letters. Then ask the students,

"Has anyone figured out the secret word—the one word we can make that uses all our letters?"

Explain that some days students will be able to figure out the word, but other days they might not. Tell them that when they figure it out, they should keep it a secret until you ask them to make the secret word. Then direct the students to try and discover the secret word by saying,

"Take a minute now to move your letters around and see if you can make a word that uses all the letters."

Give the children a minute to see if anyone can come up with the word—not likely if this is the very first lesson, but possible. If anyone makes the word, send the child to the pocket chart and have him make the word. If not, tell the students that the word is **hands**. The students say **hands** slowly, and then one student is chosen to spell **hands** in the pocket chart with the big letters. Place the card with the word **hands** on it in the pocket chart. All the students use their letters to make the word **hands** and then spell it aloud to end this part of the lesson.

Step Two—Sorting the Words

Once the children get in the swing of making words, the Step One of the lesson should take no more than 15 minutes. That leaves 5 minutes at the end of each Making Words lesson for sorting words into patterns and using these patterns to read and spell a few new words.

For the first several lessons, however, when the children are learning how to manipulate the letters and make words, making the words might take the whole 20 minutes. In that case, most teachers do the sorting and transfer step during Words time the following day. There is no sense in trying to sort and transfer if their attention span is exhausted! After five or six lessons, however, you should pace the lesson so that the words get made in 15 minutes and the remaining 5 minutes each day are spent sorting for patterns and using these patterns to read and spell a few new words.

11. Now direct the students' attention to the words on index cards in the pocket chart and have them sort the words for patterns—which at this time of the year are beginning letters and rhymes. Early in the year, you direct the sort, but as the year goes on the children should start to look for patterns. The first day, choose the word **sad** and ask students to find another word that begins with the letter **s**.

Have a child go to the pocket chart and place **sand** under **sad**. You and children should pronounce **sad** and **sand** and decide that they begin the with same letter and the same sound. Repeat the procedure for the words **has**, **had**, **hand**, and **hands**.

12. Next, pull out the word **and** from the pocket chart and ask for someone who can find two words that end in the letters **a-n-d**.

Have a child place **sand** and **hand** under **and** in the pocket chart. You and the children should pronounce the words and decide that they all end with the letters **a-n-d** and that they all rhyme. The same procedure is used with the words **an/Dan** and **had/sad**.

Step Three—Transferring the Words

Finally, when all the rhyming words are sorted out, say, "When you are reading, you will see lots of words that end in **ad**, **an**, or **and**, and you can figure them out on your own if you think about how words with the same vowel and ending letter usually rhyme. What if you were reading and came to these words?"

Write the words **can** and **land** on index cards without pronouncing them. Have children put the index cards in the pocket chart so each word is matched to its rhyming words. The children will then use the rhyming words to figure out new words.

Say, "Thinking of a rhyming word can help you when you are writing, too. What if you were writing and needed to figure out how to spell **mad** or **band**?"

The children decide that **mad** rhymes with **had** and **sad**. **Mad** is written on an index card and placed under **had** and **sad**. Next, **band** is spelled and then placed under **sand** and **hand**.

How Making Words Is Multilevel

Making Words has become enormously popular with teachers and children. **Children love manipulating the letters, trying to figure out the secret word and finding the patterns.** Making Words works for children because (if your pacing is brisk!) they are all active, engaged, and successful! **Teachers like Making Words because they can see all levels of children growing in their word knowledge.** Every lesson begins with some short easy words, and with each progressively-challenging word the teacher uses the pocket chart letters to make sure everyone has spelled the word correctly.

- In these early lessons, some of the struggling students are still learning to identify letters and developing concepts such as first letter, last letter, beginning of word, and end of word. They are still developing their phonemic awareness and learning that sounds in words can be manipulated. Making Words lessons let them succeed and practice on their own individual levels.

- For most beginning first-graders, Making Words is an activity through which they are learning letter-sound relationships by stretching out words and hearing themselves making the sounds and trying to match them to a limited set of letters. As they sort for beginning sounds and rhymes, they develop an understanding of how words work.

- Every first-grade class, however, contains some children whose letter-sound knowledge is advanced beyond simple beginning sounds and rhyming concepts. These children are always eager to figure out the secret word and as they try to do this, they are working with concepts well beyond initial sound and rhyme. It is also for these children that every Making Words lesson (even the first one) ends with a transfer step in which the teacher shows students how the patterns in the words can help them figure out other words students will encounter in their reading and writing.

Children enter first grade with all different levels of word knowledge. Making Words activities allow the whole range of children to make discoveries about words.

More Making Words Lessons: Five-Letters with One Vowel

One of the most difficult decisions teachers make is when to move on to more-difficult formats. Our observations tell us that some teachers move too fast, leaving a trail of struggling kids behind, while others (fearing to lose their students) never move! Finding some kind of middle ground is often easier said than done!

Before moving to Making Words lessons with 5-8 letters (including two vowels), children in first grade need some practice with fewer letters and just one vowel to help them learn that there are vowels and what the vowels are. **Initial lessons should also avoid silent letters and letter combinations such as** *ch* **and** *sh*, **because early in the year children need to learn that if you stretch out words, you can hear a lot of the letters. This under-standing really moves them along in their ability to spell words while writing.**

The following page presents four more lessons with the vowel **a** (bringing the total to five) and three lessons each for **e**, **i**, **o**, and **u**. In most first grades, after doing the five lessons with **a**, *everyone* would know that **a** is a vowel and would be able to spell the two-letter words **at**, **as**, **am**, and **an**. By doing three lessons for the other vowels—a total of 17 five-letter Making Words lessons with one vowel— *everyone* in most first grade classes would be confident enough to move on to bigger words with two or more vowels.

Some classes may not need this many single-vowel lessons and can move right on into some of the lessons included in the December chapter, but remember that your word wizards are being challenged to figure out the big word and use the rhyming patterns to read and spell new words. Because even these easier lessons are quite multilevel, you should not feel too pushed to move on too soon!

For additional Making Words lists and suggestions, refer to *Making Words*, by Cunningham & Hall (Good Apple, 1994), as well as *Making More Words*, by Cunningham & Hall (Good Apple, 1997).

One-Vowel Lessons:

Letters: a l m p s
Make: am Sam Pam map lap slap slam lamp lamps
Sort for: s l -am -ap
Transfer Words: tap ham nap jam

Letters: a l n p s
Make: an pan nap lap slap snap plan plans
Sort for s p -an -ap
Transfer Words: man cap map tan

Letters: a b l s t
Make: as at lab tab sat bat bats stab last blast
Sort for: l b -ab -at -ast
Transfer Words: cab fast past rat

Letters: a m r s t
Make: am at rat mat sat Sam ram tram smart
Sort for: s r -at -am
Transfer Words: bat hat ham cat

Letters: e n r s t
Make: ten set net nest rest sent rent rents
Sort for: r n s -est -et -ent
Transfer Words: tent bet bent best

Letters: e n p s t
Make: net set pet pets pest nest sent spent
Sort for: n s p -et -ent -est
Transfer Words: vet vent vest rest

Letters: e l p s t
Make: let set pet pets step pest pelt pelts slept (2 secret words!)
Sort for: p s -et
Transfer Words: bet wet vet jet

Letters: i g n s w
Make: in sin win wins sing wing wings swing (2 secret words!)
Sort for: s w -in -ing
Transfer Words: fin ring pin ping

Letters: i p r s t
Make: is it pit sit sip tip rip trip trips strip (2 secret words!)
Sort for: s t -ip -it
Transfer Words: bit hip kit zip

Letters: i m n s t
Make: is it in tin sin sit Tim mint mints
Sort for: m t -it -in
Transfer Words: fin pin hit bit

Letters: o f n r t
Make: or on no not rot for fort front
Sort for: f n -ot
Transfer Words: got hot lot pot

Letters: o d n p s
Make: so no on Don nod pod pods nods pond ponds
Sort for: n p -od -on -o
Transfer Words: rod go Ron con

Letters: o g n r s t
Make: so go got not rot rots song strong
Sort for: s r -ong -ot
Transfer Words: no lot hot long

Letters: u h r s t
Make: us rut hut huts ruts rust hurt hurts
Sort for: h r -ut
Transfer Words: but cut nut gut

Letters: u n r s t
Make: us sun run rut nut nuts stun turn turns
Sort for: s t r -un -ut
Transfer Words: cut bun but fun

Letters: u b c r s
Make: us bus sub cub rub rubs cubs curb curbs scrub (2 secret words)
Sort for: c s r -us -ub
Transfer Words: tub Gus hub club

TONGUE TWISTERS

20 min.

GUESS THE COVERED WORD

20 min.

While the Making Words activities will be fun for students, be sure that on some days you use your 20-25 minutes after Word Wall for Tongue Twisters or Guess the Covered Word activities.

Continue to use Tongue Twisters to review beginning consonant sounds. While the Making Words activities are certainly challenging, some children may need the more straightforward reinforcement of letters and sounds that Tongue Twisters offer. More advanced students can use this opportunity to practice their dexterity with language.

Some children never become really good at putting sounds together to decode a word, but most words can be figured out by students if they look at the beginning letters, the length of the word, and they think about what word would make sense there. It is this cross-checking ability that Guess The Covered Word activities help children develop. For some children, this is their most successful decoding activity. Here are just a few of the many possible sentences that can be used. Remember to include the names of your children and relate your sentences to students' interests.

Carol likes to play **soccer**.

Kate likes to play **tennis**.

Rob likes to play **basketball**.

Juan likes to play **football**.

Susanne likes to go to the **mall**.

Corinda likes to go to the **circus**.

Brent likes to go to the **park**.

Bobby likes to go to the **fair**.

ASSESSING PROGRESS

The end of November is the time to review the performance of those children whose end-of-October assessment indicated difficulty with print concepts, phonemic awareness, word learning, or letter name and sound knowledge.

In most first grade classrooms in which teachers focused some attention on these areas with particular children during daily reading, writing, Word Wall and other word activities, even children who were struggling would be making visible progress in these areas. Remember that it is **progress** you are assessing. Some children are going to take longer than other children to develop these abilities, but if we see month-to-month progress based on your nudges during daily activities, you know that children will eventually develop these critical understandings. For children who are making progress, but are still below the average ability level of your class, continue the kind of individual nudging you have been doing for as long as necessary.

Our experience with "won't give up" teachers tells us that all first graders can eventually develop print concepts and phonemic awareness and learn some words, letter names and sounds. The question is not "If?" but "When?" and the answer depends on your willpower and determination to continue to assess and nudge.

DECEMBER

December in first grade seems to fly like the snow that falls in many parts of the world. It is hard to keep to any kind of a schedule and get the routine things done. By this time of the year Word Wall activities put a sparkle in children's eyes. Creative teachers have found a way to make this fast paced and highly motivating.

First graders love to clap, snap, slide, cheer, whisper, and write the words in the air and on paper. It's definitely multisensory with students looking at the words (visual), spelling and saying the words (auditory), as well as writing and clapping them (kinesthetic).

During December, continue to introduce and practice Word Wall words and to do related Word activities each day. This month we will expand upon and increase the difficulty level of activities with which children have already become familiar.

By the end of December, you will have introduced the following:

- Theme or holiday theme boards (containing pictures and words) as a source for spelling words
- Theme board words in Guess the Covered Word activities
- Special letter combinations (the digraphs **sh**, **ch**, **th**, and **wh**) in Tongue Twisters and Guess the Covered Word activities

- Making Words lessons with an increased difficulty level (6-8 letters)
- Expanded Making Words lessons that match your class's stories and themes

WORD WALL/ THEME BOARD

10 min.

ON-THE-BACK ACTIVITY

Continue to add five new words to the Word Wall each week. In addition to the Word Wall, most teachers have **a theme board which relates to a particular theme being studied.** The theme board contains pictures and words which relate to the theme and help children when they choose to write about that theme.

In December, you might have a Happy Holidays theme board in your classroom that contains pictures and words such as:

Christmas	**Hanukkah**
Kwanzaa	**New Year's**
holiday	**December**
cold	**winter**
tree	**presents**
Santa	**sleigh**
snow	**decorations**
dreidel	**party**
celebrate	**cookies**

and/or other words appropriate for your children.

Combine students' word-wall practice with sentence-writing. Have students turn their Word Wall papers over and then dictate one or two sentences that are made up of words from your Word Wall *and* the theme board. Depending on what words you have on the wall and the theme board, you might include sentences such as:

Winter starts in December.

We have a Christmas tree.

Some people celebrate Kwanzaa in December.

Some people celebrate Hanukkah in December.

Some people celebrate Christmas in December.

Children love to write about the holidays, and learning how to use words from the theme board and the Word Wall to write sentences will help them develop their independent writing ability.

TONGUE TWISTERS WITH *SH, CH, TH,* AND *WH*

15 min.

Once children have started using what they know about beginning letters to help them read and write words, they should learn some special letter combinations. The best way to teach children the **sh, ch, th,** and **wh** letter combinations is to present some key words that begin with the letters. If you have children such as Sheila and Chuck in your room, you may already have example words for these sounds on your Word Wall. If not, you may want to add the words **she, thing, what,** and **children** to the Word Wall before introducing these special sounds. Once the children can read and spell words that begin with the letter combinations, they can associate the sounds with these known words.

If children have enjoyed the other tongue twisters, you may want to add some like these:

<u>Ch</u>ildren <u>ch</u>eer for <u>ch</u>eeseburgers and <u>ch</u>ocolate.

<u>Th</u>adeus <u>th</u>umped <u>Th</u>elma's <u>th</u>umb.

<u>Wh</u>itney <u>wh</u>istles at <u>wh</u>eels and <u>wh</u>ales.

<u>Sh</u>erry <u>sh</u>ivers when <u>sh</u>e <u>sh</u>owers.

For each Tongue Twister, underline the first two letters (**sh, ch, th** or **wh**) in each word. Help children to realize that in each case the two letters have a special sound which is very different from the sounds they have when they are by themselves. You should probably also point out (especially if the word **Christmas** is all over the room!) that **ch** usually has the sound you hear at the beginning of **children** but can also have the sound you hear at the beginning of **Christmas**.

GUESS THE COVERED WORD WITH *SH, CH, TH,* AND *WH*

15 min.

Continue presenting Guess the Covered Word lessons to your students as described in the October section (see pages 34-35), but now include words with **s**, **sh**, **c**, **ch**, **t**, **th**, **w**, and **wh**. When the beginning sound is **sh**, **ch**, **th**, or **wh**, have your first piece of paper cover both these letters. Here are some starters.

People

Carol saw a **seal.**

Roberta saw a **shark**.

Bob likes **cartoons**.

Pedro sits in the **chair.**

Rachel broke her **toe**.

Rasheed broke his **thumb**.

In Our Room

Teddy worked at a **table.**

Sue looked at the **thermometer.**

See the pictures in the **window.**

Teachers use **chalk.**

Let's sit on the **carpet.**

Clean up the mess in the **sink.**

Look at the books on the **shelf.**

At the Fair

Ride the **cars.**

Buy some **tickets.**

Are you **thirsty**?

Spin the **wheel!**

Throw the dart and be a **winner.**

I lost my **shoe.**

Presents

Bob wants a **watch.**

Bo needs a **thermos.**

Rachel wants a **phone.**

Kathy asked for a **shirt.**

Pedro asked for a **sailboat.**

CJ wants a set of **checkers.**

Things to Eat

Do you like **watermelon**?

I like bread made from **wheat**.

Cindy likes orange **sherbet**.

Do you like **salmon**?

CJ wants some **chocolate**.

I want a **taco**.

MAKING WORDS

20 min.

If you started Making Words in November and did a number of lessons with five letters and just one vowel, the children are now probably ready to move on to lessons that have 5-8 letters, including two vowels. As you present these lessons you should do less cueing than you did in early lessons. For example, in early lessons, you may have said, "Change the *last* letter . . ." As the students progress, they should be the ones thinking about what letter to change, and your direction should be limited to something such as, "Change just one letter..."

Teaching a Sample Making Words Lesson

Step One—Making Words

Here is an example of a great December lesson with six letters (two of which are vowels) as it is presented with less cueing:

The children have the letters: **e, i, n, r, t, w**

"Take two letters and make the word **in**. Say **in** with me."

"Add a letter to make the three-letter word, **tin**. Some cans are made of **tin**. Let's all say **tin**."

"Now change the vowel and **tin** will become **ten**. You have **ten** fingers and **ten** toes. Say **ten**."

"Move the letters in **ten** around to turn your **ten** into a **net**. He caught the fish in a **net**. Say **net**."

"Now change just one letter and **net** can become **wet**. When it's raining, you get **wet**. Say **wet**."

"The last three-letter word we'll make is **win**. Will he **win** the race? Say **win**."

"Now we are going to make some four-letter words. Hold up four fingers. Add one letter to **win** and you will have **twin**. My friend has a **twin** sister. Stretch out the word **twin** and listen to the sounds you hear yourself saying."

"Take all your letters out of your holder and start over. Make another four letter word—**went**. We **went** swimming today. Everyone say **went**."

"Now change just one letter and **went** can become **rent**. I paid the **rent**. Let's all say **rent**."

"The next one is a four-letter word but only has three letters that you can hear. Make **tire**. My bike had a flat **tire**. See if you can figure out what letter is in the word **tire** but isn't heard when you say the word. Let's all say **tire**."

"Now change just one letter and **tire** can become **wire**. Find the yellow **wire**. Say **wire**."

"Now let's make a five-letter word. Hold up five fingers! Use five letters to spell **twine**. **Twine** is a heavy string we use to tie things. Everyone say **twine**."

"Has anyone figured out the secret word?" (Give children one minute to try to make the word.) "The secret word is **winter**. **Winter** starts in December. Use all your letters to make **winter**. Say **winter** and stretch it out so you can hear all the letters."

Step Two—Sorting Words

After the children have made the secret word, have them use the large word cards to sort for a variety of patterns. Begin with the word **win** and have them find the other words that begin with **w**—**wet**, **went**, **wire**, and **winter**. As each word is identified, let a child place the word card in the pocket chart.

Now place the card with the word **tin** in the pocket chart and have students find the other words that begin with **t**—**ten**, **twin**, **tire**, and **twine**. Separate the **t** words into two groups—one with **tin**, **ten**, and **tire**, and the other with **twin** and **twine**. Have students notice that **twin** and **twine** begin with **tw** and that if you stretch the words out you can hear both letters.

Next help them to sort the words into rhymes:

in	net	rent	tire
tin	wet	went	wire
win			
twin			

Step Three—Transferring Words

Remind the children that knowing some words can help them read and spell the rhyming words. Write a few words and have children use the rhymes they have already sorted to decode them:

    fire   jet

Say a few words that rhyme with the sorted words and have students decide how they would spell the words you said:

    tent   pin

More Making Words Lessons:

Here are a few other seasonal lessons that are progressively more challenging. The first lesson has five letters with only one vowel, the next two lessons have seven letters with two vowels, and the last lesson has eight letters with two vowels.

Letters: i f g s t
Make: if is it sit fit fits fist sift gift gifts
Sort for: s f -it -ift
Transfer Words: lit sit lift shift

Letters: e e n p r s t
Make: net pet pets pest nest rest rent sent spent enter pester present (and serpent)
Sort for: n p r -et -est -ent pest-pester
Transfer Words: wet west went tent

Letters: a e c d l n s
Make: as an can Dan and sand land clan clean dance dances cleans candle candles
Sort for: c cl -an -and s pairs
Transfer Words: band man than hand

Letters: i o c g k n s t
Make: is it in ink sink sing song king tick sick sock stock sting stink stocking
Sort for: s st -ink -ing -ick -ock
Transfer Words: pink wing shock chick

Planning Your Own Making-Words Lessons

It is fun to plan Making Words lessons to fit in with themes you are studying. Here are the steps to go through to plan a lesson:

1. Decide what the "secret word" is that can be made with all the letters. In choosing this word, consider books the children are reading, and what letter-sound patterns you can draw children's attention to through the sorting and transferring steps at the end.

2. Make a list of other words students can make from these letters.

3. From all the words you could make, pick 10-15 words that include the following:

   a. Words that can be sorted for the pattern you want to emphasize
   b. Little words and big words so that the lesson is a multilevel lesson.
   c. Words that can be made by arranging the same letters in different ways (cold/clod) so that children are reminded that when spelling words, the ordering of the letters is crucial.
   d. A name or two to remind them that names need capital letters.
   e. Words that most students have in their listening vocabularies.

4. Write all the words on index cards and order them from shortest to longest.

5. Sequence the index cards so that you can emphasize letter patterns and how changing the position of the letters or changing/adding just one letter results in a different word.

6. Store the cards in an envelope. On the envelope, write the words in order, the patterns you will sort for, and several words for the transfer activity.

JANUARY

January marks the beginning of a new calendar year. It's a time to think about where we have been and where we are going in order to make our New Year's resolutions. By now, many first grade students are familiar with the words on the Word Wall and use them when writing. Some students are using the starred or stickered words on the wall to transfer the high-utility rhyming patterns to new reading and writing words. Remember to keep adding new words to your Word Wall each week.

Tongue Twisters and Guess the Covered Word have become classroom favorites. Many students are now cross-checking most of the time. Continuing these activities will allow more students to use these strategies independently.

Making Words is now effortless for you and the children, and the children look forward to guessing the secret word the moment they see the letters. The multi-level aspect insures success for all students and ALL are eager to move the letters and build new words.

Our resolution is to continue and add some new wrinkles to these activities that are so multi-level that they offer new challenges and success for all first graders. Using developmentally appropriate assessment, such as writing samples and running records, you will monitor individual progress and focus instruction for those who require additional help.

By the end of January, you will have introduced the following:

- "On-the-Back" activities with word endings
- Tongue Twisters and Guess the Covered Word activities with blends
- Making Words activities that include making, sorting, and transferring words with blends
- Use of writing samples and running records that can be used to monitor student progress

WORD WALL

10 min.

The class Word Wall should continue to grow throughout January. Most first-grade word walls would have 50-60 high-frequency words by the end of the month. If you were to watch a teacher do the daily Word Wall activity of calling out five words for the children to locate, cheer for, and write, you might conclude that all the children were learning the same thing—how to spell the words—but your conclusion would be wrong!

Word Wall is actually a multilevel activity because different children are at all different stages of their word learning. By selecting and adding high-frequency words which children have read in selections during the previous week's guided/shared-reading activities, many of the children have already learned to read the words added to the wall and they are indeed doing what it looks like they are doing—learning to spell them!

Unless your classroom is quite different from most first grades, there will be other children who have not learned to read all the Word-Wall words during the previous week's reading. Some children need a lot of practice to learn to read the important high-frequency words. After reading these words during Shared/Guided reading last week, they might be able to recognize them in the selection read but not be able to recognize them in another selection. When we call out words for the children to locate, cheer for and write, some children are getting the added practice necessary for them to eventually read these words anywhere they see them.

Once children have learned to read these high-frequency words (which might take several weeks or even months of practice), the very same Word Wall activity through which they learned to read them becomes the vehicle through which they to learn to spell them. Meanwhile, children know which words are on the wall and can locate them as they need to spell them during writing. In most classrooms, the rule is: "Spell words the best you can, but if the word is on the Word Wall, you have to spell it right!"

There are also a few children in every first grade who are such fast word learners that they learned to both read and spell the words during last week's reading of a selection in which these words occurred! What are they learning from the daily Word Wall activity? These super word learners are one of the reasons most teachers combine handwriting instruction with the writing of the Word Wall words. Even fast word learners in first grade need reminders and modelling of how to make the letters so that their writing can be easily read. The related On-the-Back activity also helps even the fastest word learners.

ON-THE-BACK ACTIVITY

5 min.

Spelling Rhyming Words

As earlier chapters have pointed out, children can use Word Wall words to help them read and spell lots of rhyming words. At least one day a week (for the remainder of the year), your class Word Wall activities should include an On-the-Back activity such as the following:

"You can use all the Word Wall words to help you spell when you are writing. The reason we are putting these words on the Word Wall is because they are words you see over and over in books, and they are words that you use over and over when you are writing. It would be impossible to read and write without knowing our Word Wall words. Some of the Word Wall words [starred or stickered in most classrooms] are particularly helpful words because they help you spell lots of rhyming words. Let's work on that today. One of the Word Wall words you practiced today was **eat**. I am going to say some sentences you might want to write that have words that rhyme with **eat**. Listen for the rhyming word and then we will decide together how to spell that word. What if you wanted to write:

My team **beat** the other team.

Yes, the word that rhymes with **eat** is **beat**, and we know that words that rhyme usually have the same spelling pattern. Let's write the first letter **b**. Since the word **eat** is a short word that starts with a vowel, the whole word is the spelling pattern. Add **e-a-t** to the **b** to spell the rhyming word **beat**."

The lesson continues with the teacher saying one sentence at a time, where each sentence includes one word that rhymes with **eat** and has the **e-a-t** spelling pattern.

"We had a storm and the **heat** was off at my house.

We had company and I had to get my room clean and **neat**.

I was good at school so my Dad took me to the mall for a **treat**.

Some kids will **cheat** to win a game."

Note that some rhyming words have different spelling patterns. This is precisely the reason why *you* provide students with rhyming words rather than asking *them* to give you examples. Students need to learn that most rhyming words have the same spelling pattern. If you ask students for words that rhyme with **eat**, they are apt to volunteer **feet** or **street**, and then they won't understand why the spelling patterns don't match. Later, they will learn that some rhymes have two possible spelling patterns and they just have to remember which one to use, but **at this point in first grade, the goal is for students to realize that spelling is not letter-by-letter but rather is related to patterns.**

A first grader who uses patterns to spell **street** as **s-t-r-e-a-t** is way ahead of most first graders who would work letter-by-letter and spell it **s-t-r-e-t**. **This activity moves the good word learners along in their ability to decode and spell words not yet learned. It is also good phonemic awareness training for children still struggling with the oral concept of rhyme.**

ON-THE-BACK ACTIVITY

5 min.

Adding Endings to Words

Another On-the-Back activity you might want to introduce this month is how to spell Word-Wall words that have endings. Imagine that the five Word Wall words you called out for students to locate, cheer for, and write were:

want   eat   look   talk   play

Have students turn their papers over and give them directions such as the following:

"Today we are going to practice spelling these Word Wall words when they have endings added to them. I will start by saying some sentences. Listen for the Word Wall word that has an ending added in each sentence.

My friends and I love **eating** at McDonald's.

We were **looking** for some new shoes.

I was **talking** on the phone to my Grandma.

My mom **wants** the new baby to be a girl.

My friend spent the night and we **played** Nintendo until 11:00."

As another example, review the following five Word Wall words and each sentence with an ending added to one of the words:

go   want   tell   give   ride

I am **going** to buy some new clothes.

My brother **wanted** a new computer.

Sue is **telling** her mom goodbye.

Doris **gives** away lots of books.

Bo **rides** his bike around the block.

After each sentence, the children identify the Word Wall word and the ending, decide how to spell it, and write it on their papers. **This activity uses all three endings first graders need to learn—s, ed, and ing.** On some days, you might focus on just one ending. These endings do not require any spelling changes to the Word Wall words. Later in the year the activity can include Word Wall words that needed to have an **e** dropped, a **y** changed to an **i**, or a letter doubled when an ending is added. By deciding ahead of time what words (and what endings) will be used, you will be able to control when and how students learn about changing letters when adding endings. Learning how to spell words with a variety of endings and spelling changes really moves the accelerated learners along in their writing ability.

TONGUE TWISTERS WITH BLENDS

15 min.

By January, most first graders can associate sounds with single letters and with **sh**, **ch**, **th**, and **wh**. There is one more group of beginning letters to which children need to pay attention—two- and three-letter blends. In these blends, you can hear the individual sound of each letter but they are difficult for children to separate. In fact if you look at their invented spelling, you will often see **jop** for **drop** and many **sn/sm** and **fl/fr** confusions. Focusing on the blends can take many forms and can easily be incorporated with word activities you are currently doing. If the children have enjoyed learning and illustrating tongue twisters, you might want to have them learn some for the blends. Here are some examples to get you started. Be sure to adapt the content and the names you use to fit your children where appropriate. Underline the blends just like you did for the digraphs learned last month.

Blondie's blueberries bloomed and blossomed.

Bruce's brother Brian brought brown bread for breakfast.

Claudia closed the closet full of clean clothes.

Crabs, crickets and crocodiles are creepy creatures.

Drew draws dragons dropping drinks.

Flags flip, fly, and flutter.

Freddie and Fran fry French fries.

Gloria's glum because she glued her glasses.

Slick Sly slept on his slippery sled.

Smart Smitty smells smoke.

Snoopy the snail snatched the snake's snazzy sneakers.

Sparky speeded into space on a special spaceship.

Stephanie Stegasaurus stepped on Steven's stuff.

Swans swim, swirl, swoop, and sway.

Tracy tripped over Trey's trucks and trains.

Skinny Skunk skipped over a skeleton.

GUESS THE COVERED WORD WITH BLENDS

20 min.

When presenting Guess the Covered Word sentences to your students, include some covered words that each begin with a single letter and others that each begin with two or more letters that can be heard if the word is said slowly. Be sure that when you uncover the beginning letters, you uncover **all** the letters in front of the vowel.

If you have uncovered an **s** and a child guesses the word **snow**, tell the child that that was good thinking for the **s**. Then, have everyone say **snow** slowly so that they hear the **n**. Remind students that when you uncover the beginning letters, you reveal all the letters in front of the vowel. If the word were **snow** there would also be an **n** revealed.

Use sentences such as the following to help students cue their guesses to the number of beginning letters revealed:

Justin likes to play ball in the **summer**.

Carlos likes to play in the **snow**.

Manuel likes to **skate**.

Katrin likes **snakes**.

Val likes to play all kinds of **sports**.

Kevin heard a **cricket** chirp.

Sarah heard loud **clapping**.

Paula heard a baby **cry**.

Louis heard a **cat** fight.

Carol heard a loud **blast**.

Sherika heard a **bluebird** singing.

Bob was very **brave** when he went to the hospital.

Carlton goes fishing off the **bridge**.

Bob was camping and saw a black **bear**.

Bo made a **snowman**.

Alexis wore a red **scarf**.

Help Sally **dry** the dishes.

The kitten likes to play with **string**.

Susan's favorite season is **spring**.

MAKING WORDS WITH BLENDS

20 min.

The Making Words activities that were chosen in December had secret words that fit in with a theme, unit, or seasonal activity. Another reason for choosing particular activities is to include specific examples for which to sort. The Making Words lessons for January have all been selected because the words in each lesson begin with a two-letter blend or with one of the two letters in the blend.

Step One—Work with the students to **make each chosen word** in their holders and in the pocket chart.

Step Two—For each lesson, after students have made the words, have them **sort the words** according to their beginning letters—everything in front of the vowel. Then say some other words that begin with the blend or with one of the other letters and have children decide how they would begin to spell each of the words. Next, have students sort the words by their rhymes.

Step Three—Once the words have been sorted and the rhymes have been checked, give the students the **rhyming transfer words** to read and spell. Like the words the students made in the lesson, the emphasis of the transfer words is on blends.

Letters: a e b c h n r s
Make: Ben ban ran bran barn race brace beach reach ranch branch ranches branches
Sort for: b r br; -an -ace -anch -each
Transfer Words: plan teach trace place

Letters: e i b d g r
Make: be bed red rid bid big rig brig bred bird ride bride ridge bridge
Sort for: b r br; -ed -id -ig -ide -idge
Transfer Words: sled slid slide twig

Letters: a e l n p s t
Make: pat pet let pan plan pant past last lane late plate plane plant planet planets
Sort for: p l pl; -an -ant -ast -ate -ane
Transfer Words: chant blast date fast

Letters: e u d n s s t t
Make: ten sun stun stud suds send sent tent tend test tents stunt student students
Sort for: s t st; -un -end -ent
Transfer Words: spend spent fun trend

Letters: a e c c k r r s
Make: car care cake rake rack race racer crack creak creaks cracks crackers
Sort for: c r cr; -ake -ack
Transfer Words: shake shack black snake

Letters: e o c h l s t
Make: lot cot cost lost colt clot clots colts cloth close closet clothes
Sort for: c l cl; -ot -ost
Transfer Words: shot frost spot trot

ASSESSING PROGRESS

Good assessment is an ongoing activity. Teachers watch children in a variety of reading and writing situations and notice what strategies they are using and what they need to move them forward. Many teachers observe the progress of a different group of students each day of the week. Each student in the class will be designated by the teacher as being in one of the week's five observation groups. On Monday, the teacher's clipboard contains the anecdotal record sheets for the students designated as Monday children. The teacher writes down what is noticed about the reading and writing strategies these Monday children are using. At the end of Monday, she files away the Monday sheets and attaches to the clipboard the record sheets for the Tuesday children. **This procedure makes the notion of anecdotal records workable and also assures that no child gets "lost in the shuffle" because each child gets "noticed" on a weekly schedule.** The weekly observations of children help the teacher to present lessons that are appropriate and that provide the nudges particular children need.

In addition to the weekly observations described above, it is also good from time to time to stop and assess progress in a more systematic way. For many teachers, the halfway point in first grade is a good time to do some more systematic assessment. In spite of the fact that this book is primarily about how to teach phonics and spelling strategies in first grade, you can only assess these strategies by looking at the actual reading and writing of students. Remembering the principle "What they don't use, they don't have!" you assess students' decoding and spelling as they are actually reading and writing.

Observing Word Strategies In Reading

In observing children's reading, teachers can look at the errors or miscues that children make and determine what word identification strategies they are using. **Good readers will self-correct many of their miscues.** This usually indicates that they are using context to check that what they are reading makes sense. **Successful self-correction is an excellent indicator that the reader is using all three cueing systems—meaning (semantic), sounding like language (syntactic), and letter-sound knowledge (graphophonic) successfully.** Some readers tend to overuse context—their miscues make sense but don't have most of the letter-sound relationships of the original word. Others overuse letter-sound knowledge. Their miscues look and sound a lot like the original words but they don't make any sense. By observing children's reading, you can determine what strategies they are using and what kind of instructional activities you might provide for them.

Running Records

To look at the word strategies children use while reading, you first must have something for them to read in which they make some errors—but not too many. This level is generally referred to as instructional level—the level of a book or story in which the child correctly identifies at least 90-95% of the words and has adequate comprehension of what was read. The text the child is reading should be something the child has not read before and should be approximately 100 words in length. (For beginning readers some teachers and informal inventories use passages with 50 words.)

Teachers use a variety of materials to do this assessment—depending on what is available and what the school system requires.

- Some teachers use passages contained in the assessment package that accompanies many basal reading series.
- Other teachers or schools have designated certain "real" books as benchmark books. They use these books for assessment purposes only and not for instruction. They designate a particular book to be what most first graders could read at the 90-95% word identification accuracy level early in the year. Another book represents a difficulty level appropriate for the middle of first-grade, and a third book is selected as an appropriate level for the end of first-grade.

- In schools where Reading Recovery® is used, some first-grade teachers use books designated by Reading Recovery® scoring to be at particular levels.
- Finally, some teachers use a published Informal Reading Inventory which contains graded passages beginning at preprimer level and going through sixth grade.

Regardless of what you use, the procedures are the same. **Have the child read the text you think will be at instructional level. This text should be text the child has not had a chance to read before, and the child should be told that you cannot help her while she is reading. When she gets to a word she doesn't know, she should "do the best she can to figure it out" because you can't tell her any words. Also tell the child that she should think about what she is reading because she will be asked to use her own words to tell what the text she read was about after she has read it.**

As the child reads, keep a running record of her performance using procedures adapted from Marie Clay's (1993) system. If you have made a copy of the text because you are using a passage from a basal assessment or an Informal Reading Inventory (Johns, 1997), mark right on the passage. If not, simply use a sheet of paper to record the child's performance.

Here are examples of two different ways to record a child's reading performance of instructional-level material. The first record is on an actual copy of the passage and the second is on a running record sheet. (Of course you would only need to record it one way or the other!)

Running Record with Text

from *The Biggest Sandwich Ever*
by Jeffrey Stoodt (Steck-Vaughn, 1997)

✓   ✓ ✓ ✓   ✓   ✓
Long ago, a very little town
✓ ✓   ✓   ✓
made the biggest sandwich (around.)

✓ ✓   ✓ ✓   ✓ ✓   ✓
The jolly baker had so much fun
✓   ✓ good   ✓   sc
making a giant sandwich bun.

✓ baker bought ✓ sc ✓
The butcher brought some tasty meat,
sc ✓   ✓   ✓   ✓   ✓
piled up high, sliced and neat.

Running Record without Text

from *The Biggest Sandwich Ever*
by Jeffrey Stoodt (Steck-Vaughn, 1997)

✓   ✓ ✓ ✓   ✓   ✓

✓ ✓   ✓   ✓

(   )

✓ ✓   ✓ ✓   ✓ ✓   ✓

✓   ✓ good   ✓   sc
          giant

✓ baker bought   ✓ sc ✓
   butcher brought
sc ✓   ✓   ✓   ✓   ✓

As you can tell from the sample, a simple marking system is used. Note that only the first 100 words are scored (even though the passage read might be somewhat longer or shorter).

- Put a check mark (✓) over each word read correctly.

- If the child misreads a word (such as **good** for **giant**) write the error above the word.

- If the child leaves a word out, circle that word.

- If the child self-corrects, write **sc** above it. Self-corrected words are counted as correct.

- If the child makes the same error more than once, only count it one time.

- After the child has read the passage, have the child close the book (or put the passage away) and ask the child to explain what the text was about. Ask questions as needed to determine that the child understood at least 70-80% of the information read.

In the example, the child misread or left out five words, giving that child a word identification accuracy rate of 95%. Comprehension was adequate. The passage appears to be at the instructional level of the child. The child's errors and self corrections can now be analyzed to determine what word strategies the child is actually using. (If you wanted to determine the highest level at which this child could read, you would need to have the child continue reading higher and higher passages until word identification accuracy drops below the 90-95% level or comprehension falls below the 70-80% level.)

Looking at the words read correctly, errors and self-corrections, you would know that:

The child is developing a store of high-frequency words since Word Wall words are being read correctly. (including the words **the**, **had**, **fun**, **some**, **made**, **up**, **all**, and **then**)

The child is cross-checking meaning and letter sounds since the self-corrections were probably triggered by the meaning of the words in the sentence made after the initial error. (**but** was said first, then was self-corrected to **bun**)

The child is using initial letter knowledge since the three words miscalled all began with the correct letters. (**baker–butcher**, **good–giant**, and **bought–brought**)

The child seems less sure about what to do with big words since some words the child had difficulty with were polysyllabic words. (**around** and **baker**)

Since this passage was determined by this teacher to be "about right" for mid-first grade, you can determine that at this level, the child is applying what he knows about sight words, meaning, and letter-sounds while reading.

Imagine, however, that on this passage, the child being assessed had only made one error—giving him a word identification accuracy rate of 99%—and had adequate comprehension. You could, of course, be pleased because if this passage is about right for most children in the middle of first-grade, the child being assessed is a better than average reader. But, what can you tell about that child's decoding? You might just decide that this child is moving along fine and that you don't need to know anymore. If you did feel the need to assess the child's decoding, however, you would need to find a passage for him in which his word identification accuracy was in the 90-95% range so that you could see what strategies are used for decoding unknown words.

On the other hand, imagine that the child makes 15 errors on this middle-of first grade passage. When a child is making that many errors, it is impossible to cross check meaning and letter-sounds, etc., because so much of the meaning is missing in all the words left out or miscalled. You can't make judgements about the child's decoding-while-reading abilities until you have the child reading a passage at the instructional level. You need to find a text where the child's word-identification accuracy is at the 90-95% level and comprehension is adequate and analyze the errors on that passage. Of course, midway through first grade, you may not be able to find a new passage that the child has never read before which is at instructional level. For these children, we will have to rely on our daily observations and your analysis of word development in their writing and spelling until they develop an instructional reading level.

Observing Word Strategies In Writing

Writing samples also show growth in word knowledge. Because writing results in a visible, external product, it is easier to determine what students are actually using. When looking at a student's writing samples to determine his level of word knowledge, look at his spelling of high-frequency words and his attempts at spelling unfamiliar words.

Here is a sample written by one first grader in January. Boldfaced words are all from the Word Wall. The words in boxes were not on the Word Wall but were displayed on theme boards or in other places in the room. The remaining words are words the child spelled as best he could. Circled words are words the child circled which he believes are not spelled correctly.

David's Writing Sample

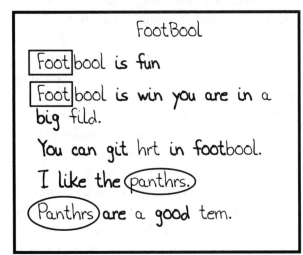

What can you tell about David's developing word knowledge by looking at this sample? First notice that all the Word Wall words (except **get** and **when**) are spelled correctly. The fact that the boxed words are also spelled correctly shows that the child knows how to use the print in the room to help spell words.

Next, look at how the child is spelling words not apt to be known by a first grader and not readily available in the room. This child spelled:

> **ball–bool**
>
> **get–git**
>
> **hurt–hrt**
>
> **team–tem**

These are very good attempts at spelling and show that the child is able to hear sounds in words and knows what letters usually represent those sounds. His spelling of **panthrs** shows the development of some knowledge of spelling patterns (**panthrs** may be based on the child's knowledge of the sound and spelling of the word **can**).

The next sample was written by a highly-literate first grader in January.

Michelle's Writing Sample

Polobears

I like polobears because they slide down the ice. They are white as snow. The baby polobears are cute. When I went to the zoo with my class we saw some polobears in the water. Polobears are probroly soft. I would like to pet a polobear if I could. But I can't because my mom won't let me pet one. I really really like polobears.

All of the Word Wall words (underlined) are spelled correctly. Throughout the sample only a few words are misspelled, and these incorrect spellings still show a sophisticated understanding of letters, sounds, and spelling patterns.

Finally, we have included a January writing sample from a child who is still struggling with words and spelling.

Rachel's Writing Sample

kiderqoten

kederqoten is relley fun.

win I wus in kiderqodin I wus in two klasis.

One wus in Floridu and one wus in Not Carulinu.

Not all the words from the Word Wall (underlined) are spelled correctly—but most are. This child does know where to look for words in the room as evidenced by the number of underlined words spelled correctly. Although this child's word knowledge is not where you might expect the average first grader to be at this point of first grade, almost all the words are decipherable by an experienced reader of children's spelling attempts.

In addition to writings on self-selected topics, many schools collect focused writing samples and look at these to determine growth in writing ability and word knowledge. A focused writing sample collected for assessment purposes should have a topic specified about which most children have good general knowledge. Children should write on the topic with no assistance from the teacher or any other child. Some examples of topics used in primary classrooms include:

My Favorite Things To Do

What I Like to Do at School

An Animal I Would Like to Have for a Pet

Many schools have the child write about the same topic at several different points in time—May of kindergarten, January and May of first grade, and January and May of second grade, for example. These topic-focused, non-assisted first drafts are then compared to determine an individual child's writing growth. In addition to a slew of valuable information about how the child writes—sentence sense, topic sense, word choice, writing conventions, etc.—these samples yield valuable information about the child's developing word knowledge.

Observing Word Strategies for Spelling Unknown Words

Finally, there is one more quick and simple measure that can be used at the midway point of first grade to determine how children are developing their word knowledge. Making sure that each child cannot see what others are writing, we dictate ten words to them which we don't expect them to be able to spell and then analyze their attempts. Teachers use a variety of words, the major criterion being that these words are not (and have not been) available in the room and that they present a variety of different patterns. Many teachers use the following ten words, suggested by Gentry (1987) and Gentry and Gillet (1993) on their Developmental Spelling Test:

monster

united

dress

bottom

hiked

human

eagle

closed

bumped

type

(If your children like to write about monsters and thus have learned to spell **monster**, you might substitute another word, perhaps **blister** or **mountain**.)

Once children have spelled the ten words as best they can, Gentry and Gillet suggest analyzing their spelling using the following stages:

The Precommunicative Stage: Spelling at this stage contains scribbles, circles, and lines with a few letters thrown in at random. These letters are usually just there and any connection between these letters and the words they are thinking is pure coincidence.

The Semiphonetic Stage: The second stage can be seen when words begin to be represented by a letter or two. The word **monster** may be written with just an **m** or an **mr** or a **mtr**. **Type** might be written with just a **t** or **tp**. This stage indicates that the child is beginning to understand letter-sound relationships and knows the consonant letters which represent some sounds.

The Phonetic Stage: In the third stage, vowels appear—not necessarily always the right vowels but vowels are used and most sounds are represented by at least one letter. Phonetic spellings of **monster** might include **munstr** and **mostr**. **Type** will probably be spelled **tip**. You can usually tell when a child is in the phonetic stage because you can read most of what children in this stage write.

The Transitional Stage: In this stage all sounds are represented and the spelling is usually a possible English spelling, just not the correct spelling. **Monster** in this stage might be spelled **monstir** or **monstur**. **Type** is probably spelled **tipe**.

The Conventional Stage: Finally, the child reaches the stage of conventional spelling in which most words which a child at that grade level could be expected to spell correctly are spelled correctly.

Of course, children's spelling of different words will indicate different stages. The important thing is not which stage they are in but how they are growing. Put the sample away along with writing samples and running records and use them to compare how they do on the very same tasks toward the end of the year.

Children come to us on all different literacy and word levels, and they develop their literacy and word abilities at different rates. "Grade-level" means "average." Children are not now and never will be average (and we shouldn't want them all to be)! What we can expect (and should document) is growth. **Children come to us multilevel. Our instruction and assessment must reflect this truth!**

FEBRUARY

February is full of holidays and special events like Groundhog Day, Valentine's Day, President's Day, Dental Health Month, and Black History Month. These topics provide us rich opportunities to create theme boards that then allow children to explore words across the content areas.

Students will love combining Word Wall words and those fascinating big words from theme boards to build sentences.

February will include more On-the-Back, Tongue Twister, Guess the Covered Word, and Making Words activities that can support less experienced students and challenge more experienced students. A new activity, Rounding Up the Rhymes, will be introduced to focus more attention on rhymes and spelling patterns.

By the end of February, you will have introduced the following:

- Use of theme boards containing holiday pictures and words to expand reading and writing
- Student cross-checking using word length as well as beginning letters and meaning in Guess the Covered Word

- A combination of blends and word endings as a new, more advanced way to sort words during Making Words
- Rounding Up the Rhymes as a way to focus attention on spelling patterns

WORD WALL

10 min.

Continue to add words to your Word Wall. You will probably also have a February holiday board which (in addition to pictures) contains words such as: **Valentine's Day**, **cards**, **party**, **holiday**, **George Washington**, **Abraham Lincoln**, etc. Have students continue to do activities on the backs of their Word Wall papers, such as combining words from the Word Wall and the theme board to write simple sentences.

George Washington was a president.

I like Valentine's Day.

We will have a Valentine's Day party.

ON-THE-BACK ACTIVITY

5 min.

Adding Endings to Words

At least one day each week, make sure the five words you call can have endings added to them. For On-the-Back activities, dictate sentences where each sentence contains one of the words from the Word Wall with an **s**, **ed** or **ing** added to it. Students have to identify the Word Wall word and decide how to spell it with its ending. **This may be a good time to start including some words which need to have the *e* dropped before adding *ing*.** Be sure to have the children tell you that they must drop the **e** before adding **ing** before allowing anyone to write the word so that all children will have the words correctly spelled.

ON-THE-BACK ACTIVITY

5 min.

Spelling Rhyming Words

Continue to present sentences which contain words that rhyme with (and have the same spelling patterns as) one of the five Word Wall words. This activity provides a weekly opportunity for those few children who are very slow to develop phonemic awareness and a sense of oral rhyme. At the same time, it helps faster word learners spell lots of other words based on the starred or stickered Word-Wall words.

This activity is particularly useful on Monday when five new Word-Wall words are added. At least one of the new words is apt to be a starred or stickered word. Imagine, for example that the words **some, of, where, night,** and **day** are added. **Night** and **day** are the two words that have helpful spelling patterns. For this On-the-Back activity, have children write **night** on the backs of their papers and underline **i-g-h-t**. Remind children that rhyming words usually have the same spelling pattern, and then share the following sentences. Have students listen for the word in each sentence that rhymes with **night,** and then help them use **night** to spell the word.

My dog was in a **fight** with a big dog.

My dad **might** take me to the movies this Saturday.

I like to look at all the **bright** stars.

I bought new shoes because my old ones were too **tight**.

I get scared when you turn off the **light**.

After you say each sentence, let children tell you which word rhymes with **night** and what beginning letter or letters they need to use when spelling the word. Then have them write the rhyming word using the **i-g-h-t** spelling pattern.

(Notice that students are listening for rhyming words in sentences and transferring the familiar spelling pattern to their own writing of the rhyming word, but they are **not** writing the whole sentence. **Also, remember not to ask students for rhyming words because there are other words such as** *bite, quite,* **etc., with different spelling patterns that might only confuse students at this point in the year.**)

Many teachers like to use Monday and Tuesday to call out the five new words for the week for the children to write. Wednesday, Thursday, and Friday are then each used to review any five words already on the wall and their locations. If this is how you present the Word Wall words throughout the week, students will write the words **some, of, where, night,** and **day** on the front of their papers again on Tuesday. The On-the-Back rhyming activity for Tuesday could then follow Monday's example and use the word **day,** the second word with a helpful spelling pattern. Use sentences with rhyming words such as the following:

My brother was born in **May.**

You can **spray** water on the flowers with the hose.

I got a new **gray** kitten.

There is a **stray** dog that comes to my house for food.

I wanted to go out in the rain but my Mom said, "No **way!**"

GUESS THE COVERED WORD

20 min.

The year is more than half over and you might be tempted to stop doing Guess The Covered Word activities because many of your students know most of the beginning sounds in words. But, as we discussed in the January chapter (pages 66-73), children don't know something until they use it in their reading and writing. Guess the Covered Word focuses the children's attention on ALL the letters in front of the vowel—not just the first one. In addition, **Guess the Covered Word is the activity in which you teach and remind children that guessing based only on a single criteria (the first letters, the length of the word, or the word that makes sense) won't help them figure out many words in their reading. Guessing a word using all three cues is a much more reliable method and this approach will help students correctly identify the word more often than not.**

In spite of all the helpful On-the-Back rhyming activities, sorting and transferring during Making Words, and other activities, there are children who never get very good at figuring out the vowel part of the word. These children are the ones who will benefit most from the Guess the Covered Word activities, because they can become very good readers if they learn to cross-check beginning letters, length, and meaning.

Continue presenting Guess the Covered Word activities to your class until you observe the following:

- almost all the children's invented spellings have the correct beginning letters

- all guesses for unknown words during reading begin with the right letters, are about the right length, and make sense

Write sentences on the board such as the following one day out of every two weeks:

Sam would like to ride in a **helicopter**.

Roxanne would like to ride in a **spaceship**.

Justin used to ride on a **tricycle**.

Rusty can drive a **tractor**.

Gabe got a ride on a **snowplow**.

Note that each boldfaced word is the word to be guessed and is covered with two self-stick notes. The self-stick notes are cut to reveal the length of the word and the first self-stick note covers all the letters in front of the vowel.

Remember that children's natural tendency seems to be to only consider the first letter. A child who guesses **sailboat** when the **sn** of **snowplow** or the **sp** of **spaceship** has been revealed should be told: "That's a good guess for the **s** and it makes sense because you can ride in a sailboat, but **sailboat** does not have an **n**. If it did, it wouldn't be a sailboat, it would be a **snailboat**!

MAKING WORDS

20 min.

February has a few themed lessons with more than the usual 6-8 letters and 2 vowels, and also three lessons for students to review **ch**, **sh**, and **th**.

Letters: a e h r s t
Make: at hat rat ear hear tear hats rats ears hears tears earth heart hearts
Sort for: s pairs -at -ear
Transfer Words: spear spat clear flat

Letters: a e u b f r r y
Make: by buy are ear fry Ray bay bray fear year rear berry ferry February
Sort for: -ear -ay -y
Transfer Words: gear clay stray spy

Letters: a e e i l n n t v
Make: van tan tin ten net vet eat neat line nine vine vent alien invent valentine
Sort for: -an -et -eat -ine
Transfer Words: jet wheat shine than

Letters: i o c l l n n
Make: lo no on in inn ill con oil coil coin loin lion Lincoln
Sort for: -on -oin -oil
Transfer Words: join spoil Don broil

Letters: a i o g h n n s t w
Make: saw was wash want show snow sing sting swing sawing washing wanting showing snowing Washington
Sort for: ing (ending) pairs; -ing -ow
Transfer Words: glow king mow string

Letters: e e i d n p r s t
Make: see ten teen seen seed deep tree pest step steep steed pester present president
Sort for: pr; pest-pester; -ee -een -eed -eep
Transfer Words: bee queen beep feed

Letters: a i o c h m n p
Make: ham him hip hop cop cap camp chop chip chin China chain chimp champ champion
Sort for: c h ch; -champ/champion -ip -op -amp
Transfer Words: slip shop ship stamp

Letters: a o o h m p s
Make: so ho am as has ham hop hops shop shoo soap hoop hoops shampoo
Sort for: s h sh; s pairs; -am -as -op
Transfer Words: slam stop crop Pam

Letters: e u d h n r s t
Make: the ten Ted sun Sue hut shut shed then thud hunt hunts hunted hunter thunder thunders
Sort for: s t h sh th; hunt hunts hunted hunter; -en -ut
Transfer Words: men cut nut when

Do not sort for single beginning letters unless students are not using them correctly to decode words when reading or writing. Words beginning with two or more letters which have the same sound, such as **present** and **president**, should still be sorted for, as well as words with endings. When more than one word has the same ending, such as **wanting** and **washing**, pair the words with and without the endings (**want-wash** and **wanting-washing**) and pronounce and spell each pair. When an ending is added to only one word, such as **pester**, talk about how both **pest** and **pester** have the word **pest**, and explain that a pest is the person who pesters someone. Finish sorting by rhymes so students can use the spelling patterns to read and spell some transfer words.

ROUNDING UP THE RHYMES

20 min.

February is the perfect month to introduce a new Working with Words activity—Rounding up the Rhymes. This is a multilevel word activity to follow up the reading of a book, story, or poem that contains lots of rhyming words. Here is an example using the timeless book, *In a People House*, by Theodore LeSieg (Random House, 1972).

Initial Reading

The first (and often second) reading of anything should be focused on meaning and enjoyment. When you read *In A People House*, there is a lot for your students to think about and enjoy. As the mouse shows the bird what is in a people house, children encounter wonderful "Seussian" language and pictures. Mundane things such as bottles, brooms, and pillows come to life as the bird and the mouse juggle them, fly them, and fight with them! Some words and pictures may require some explanation of "life in the old days" as today's children ponder the use of a cup and **saucer**, **thread,** and **marbles**.

Identifying the Rhymes

The second or third reading of the book is an appropriate time to draw the children's attention to the wonderful rhyming words. **As you read each page or two, encourage the children to chime in and try to "hear the rhymes they are saying" (rather than asking students to listen for the rhymes as *you* say them, since children with limited phonemic awareness are much more successful hearing rhymes when they say the words and hear—and feel—themselves making the rhyme).** As children identify the rhyming words, write them on index cards and put them in a pocket chart. Some children may still be confused about what *rhyme* means and may offer words that begin alike when asked for rhyming words. Try to respond to their thinking in a way that encourages their continued participation and helps them clear up their confusion, such as with the following:

"Let's all say **piano, peanuts, popcorn,** and **pails.** That was very good listening and thinking, because **piano, peanuts, popcorn,** and **pails** do sound alike, but the sound they share is the beginning sound. Say them slowly and stretch out the words. Do you hear the **p** at the beginning? **Piano, peanuts, popcorn,** and **pails** all begin with the same sound, but they don't rhyme.

"Let's add some more words to the list. See if you can hear the rhyming words when we say them—**piano, peanuts, popcorn, pails, pencil, paper, hammer, nails.** Yes, **pails** and **nails** are the rhyming words. I will write **pails** and **nails** on these index cards and stick them in the pocket chart."

Continue having children chime in with you as you read the pages of the rhyming book until you have written six or seven sets of rhyming words on index cards and placed them in the pocket chart. If, as with *In a People House*, there are many more rhyming words, you could round up the remaining rhymes in a second rounding-up activity based on the same book. In order to avoid confusing and frustrating some children, however, you don't want more than seven sets of rhyming words for any one activity.

house	chairs	brooms
mouse	stairs	rooms
thread	door	pails
bed	more	nails
	floor	

Since the length of the lessons should not exceed 15-20 minutes, the next part of the Rounding Up the Rhymes activity usually occurs on the next day.

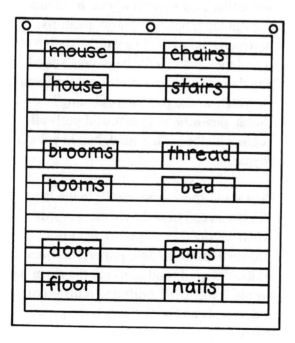

Observing Spelling Patterns

Have the children chime in on another rereading of *In a People House* and stop after each page or two to identify the rhyming words that were rounded up and put in the pocket chart on the previous day. Direct the next part of the lesson with the following:

> "Now we know that all these words rhyme. Our job today is to look very closely and see which rhyming words have the same spelling pattern."

Remind students that the spelling pattern in a short word includes all the letters beginning with the first vowel (name the vowels for the students) and going to the end of the word. Pick up the first pair of index cards with rhyming words (**mouse** and **house**), have the children identify the **o-u-s-e** spelling pattern in each, and underline the spelling pattern on each card. Explain that **house** and **mouse** rhyme and have the same spelling pattern. Emphasize that we can *hear* the rhyme and *see* the spelling pattern. Put the **house** and **mouse** cards back in the pocket chart and pick up the next set of rhymes—**chairs** and **stairs**. Repeat the steps performed with the first pair of cards. This time, the spelling pattern identified and underlined is **a-i-r-s**. Show students that the two words have the same spelling pattern and put them back in the pocket chart. Repeat the steps with the third pair of rhyming words, **brooms** and **rooms**.

Next pick up the cards with the words **thread** and **bed**. Say them with the students and help students to see that the words rhyme. Underline the **e-a-d** spelling pattern in **thread** and the **e-d** spelling pattern in **bed**. Show the students that, while the words do rhyme, they have different spelling patterns. **Remind the children that words that rhyme usually have the same spelling pattern, but sometimes rhyming words have different spelling patterns.** Tell the class that you only want to display words in your pocket chart that rhyme *and* have the same spelling pattern, and then toss **thread** and **bed** in the trash can! (Throwing these cards away is hard for some "waste not-want not" teachers to do, but doing so has a dramatic effect on the children. However, if you can't bear to trash them, just put them to one side!)

Review the spelling patterns in the words **door, more,** and **floor**, underline the spelling pattern on each card, and compare them. Return **door** and **floor** to the pocket chart and throw away **more**.

Finally, review the spelling patterns in **pails** and **nails**. Underline the spelling patterns on the cards, have the students see that they are the same, and return the cards to the pocket chart.

The pocket chart now has five sets of rhyming words with the same spelling patterns:

| h<u>ouse</u> | ch<u>airs</u> | br<u>ooms</u> | d<u>oor</u> | p<u>ails</u> |
| m<u>ouse</u> | st<u>airs</u> | r<u>ooms</u> | fl<u>oor</u> | n<u>ails</u> |

Using Spelling Patterns

In the final part of the activity, students use these words to read and write some other words. This is the transfer step and is critical to the success of this activity for children who "only learn what we teach." So far, the activity has taught what rhyming words are and that many words that rhyme have the same spelling pattern. If students aren't shown how to use this to decode and spell new words, they have not learned anything they can actually use. Begin the transfer part of this activity by telling children,

> **"You know that when you are reading books and writing stories, there are many words you have never seen before. You have to figure them out. One way many people figure out how to read and spell new words is to see if they already know any rhyming words or words that have the same spelling pattern. I am going to write some words and you can see which words with the same spelling pattern will help you read them. Then, we are going to try to spell some words by deciding if they rhyme with any of the words in our pocket chart."**

Next, write two or three words which rhyme and have the same spelling pattern as the sets of words already in the pocket chart. As you write each word on a card, have the children help you decide which letters to underline for the spelling pattern. Have a child put the card that has the new word in the pocket chart under the other words that have the same spelling pattern. Lead the class to use the rhyme to decode the word.

Finally, remind the children that thinking of rhyming words can help them spell words when they are writing. Say something like,

> "What if you were writing and wanted to tell how your new bike zooms down the road. Let's see if we can find some words in the pocket chart that rhyme with **zooms** and that probably have the same spelling pattern."

Lead the children to say **zooms** after each set of rhyming words—"**mouse, house, zooms; chairs, stairs, zooms; brooms, rooms, zooms.**" After students decide that **zooms** rhymes with **brooms** and **rooms**, let them help you to spell **zooms**. Write **zooms** on a card and put it in the pocket chart under **brooms** and **rooms**.

Here are the words rounded up from *In a People House* along with the new words read and spelled based on their rhymes and spelling patterns at the conclusion of this activity.

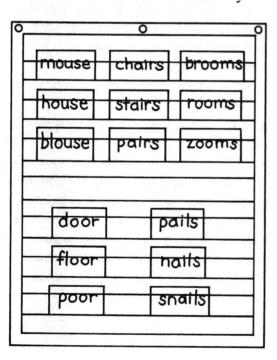

How Rounding Up the Rhymes Is Multilevel

Rounding Up the Rhymes is enormously popular with children. They all enjoy chiming in on the reading and rereading of the books. It is also a multilevel activity. Struggling readers and writers whose phonemic awareness is limited learn what rhymes are and how to distinguish rhymes from beginning sounds. Other children whose phonemic awareness is better developed learn lots of spelling patterns and also that words that rhyme often share the same spelling pattern. Our most advanced readers and writers become proficient with the strategy of using words they know to decode and spell unknown words. This proficiency shows in their increased reading fluency and in the more sophisticated nature of the invented spellings in their writing.

A serendipitous benefit for Rounding Up the Rhymes is achieved if the book used is placed with the materials available for self-selected reading. Because of the repeated readings of the books and the focus on the rhyming words, many struggling readers can fluently read the book. Books which have been read and reread and focused on for Rounding Up the Rhymes activities often become the most sought-out books in the room.

Any book with lots of rhyming words is a good candidate for a Rounding Up the Rhymes lesson. Many teachers tie this activity in with an author study of Dr. Seuss. Some of his other books that work particularly well for Rounding Up the Rhymes are *Ten Apples Up on Top* (Random House, 1961), and *One Fish, Two Fish, Red Fish, Blue Fish* (Random House, 1960).

MARCH

March is here, and with March comes spring, leprechauns, and kites. Your students are moving forward with their reading and writing, and they are having fun with the words activities that they do daily.

By this time of the year, there is a noticeable difference in the performance and confidence level of first graders as they read and write. As you continue to introduce and teach new Word Wall words, are these "springing up" in their writing?

Are your students using both context and beginning-letter sounds to cross-check the new words they meet in their daily reading? March is another month to continue to give your students an opportunity to extend their word knowledge and soar high as readers and writers through the use of Guess the Covered Word, Making Words, Rounding Up the Rhymes, and On-the-Back activities.

Remember to keep an eye out for children who may need extra help and give them the nudges they need!

By the end of March, you will have introduced the following:

- The strategy of using Word Wall words to spell new words using rhyming patterns
- More challenging On-the-Back activities where students choose from more than one spelling pattern
- Guess the Covered Word activities that include factual sentences about the students in your class

- Making Words activities with blends and with longer theme words, like **leprechaun**
- Rounding Up the Rhymes that use rhymes from read-alouds and books used in Shared/Guided Reading
- Use of Running Records or another record-keeping format to compare student writing samples–one from January and one from March

---

WORD WALL

10 min.

ON-THE-BACK ACTIVITY

10 min.

The Word Wall will probably have almost 100 words by the end of this month. The helpfulness of having this many high-frequency words instantly available to students should be obvious by the fluency with which they are writing.

> Remember that if you invest an extra 2-3 minutes in an "on-the back" activity, you can greatly increase the utility of the words displayed on your wall (and give students some additional handwriting practice and not waste the back of that half-sheet of paper).

Have students continue to practice writing Word Wall words with **s, ed,** and **ing** endings. Don't hesitate to have students put endings on words that require spelling changes. As long as you specify the spelling changes before they write the words, they can all spell them correctly. Some of the fast word learners will learn to drop the **e** when they add **ing** to **give**, **have**, **make**, **ride**, etc., and to double the **t** when they add **ing** to **get** or **quit**.

Spelling Rhyming Words

When adding a new word such as **thing** to the wall, you have the perfect opportunity to remind students that some words can help them spell lots of other words. Have them listen for the word in each of the following sentences that rhymes with **thing**:

We can **bring** our pet to school on Friday.

Spring is my favorite season because I love baseball.

When I was flying my kite, the **string** got tangled up in the trees.

We bought my Mom a **ring** for her birthday.

I broke my arm when I fell off the **swing**.

As each word is identified, each student can use the spelling pattern of the word **thing** to help him write the new word on the back of his paper.

ON-THE-BACK ACTIVITY

10 min.

Choosing from More than One Spelling Pattern

This On-the-Back rhyming activity has a format similar to the previous one, but the activity is more challenging. It allows students to choose which of the five new Word Wall words has the spelling pattern that will help them spell another word. This approach better-approximates what students actually have to do when they use the Word Wall words to help them spell a word they need while writing.

To do this rhyming activity, make sure that all the words you call out for students to write on the fronts of their papers have some words that rhyme and share the same spelling pattern. You might call out the words **make, thing, like, went,** and **will.** Help the children to notice that all these words are helpful words (and will be starred or stickered on your wall if that is how you mark them). Tell students that you are going to share some sentences and in each they will need to spell a word that rhymes with one of the five new Word Wall words. As you share each of the following sentences, emphasize the word students need to spell and let students decide which of the five new words on their papers will help to spell the new word.

We like to cook chicken on the **grill**.

I was so scared I started to **shake** all over.

My brother **spent** his whole allowance on baseball cards.

We are going to **sing** at my church on Sunday morning.

I want a new **bike** for my birthday.

Once children have begun choosing the rhyming words to help them spell new words, alternate this activity with the easier one in which your sentences use rhymes for only one of the words. The more-challenging activity will help children who are ready to learn how thinking of a rhyming word can help them spell lots of words. The easier activity allows children who are still developing their sense of rhyme to practice using spelling patterns. All children are successful when activities are multilevel.

GUESS THE COVERED WORD

15 min.

Put a slightly new twist on this (by now) old-favorite activity. Begin by selecting several students whose names you will use in the activity sentences. Instead of creating the sentences and presenting them to the class yourself, interview the children whose names you will use to create factual sentences, and then let each child present to the class the sentence that has his name in it. The child can perform each of the steps of the activity for his sentence, including calling on children for guesses before uncovering any letters, uncovering the first letters and collecting more guesses, and finally uncovering the whole word.

Sentences will be specific to the information children provide in your interviews, but may look like the following:

Michael's favorite month is **July**.

Devon's favorite sport is **football**.

Samaria's favorite food is **spaghetti**.

David's favorite day of the week is **Saturday**.

Bo likes to go to the **circus**.

Alexis likes to shop at the **mall**.

Juan wants to go to **Disneyland**.

Kim loves to go to **McDonald's**.

At the zoo CJ watched the **zebra**.

On the farm David saw some **geese**.

At the pet shop Catherine saw some **puppies**.

In the woods Julie saw a **raccoon**.

At school Amber likes to **read**.

After school Brittany likes to **tumble**.

On Saturday Bianca likes to **swim**.

On the playground Matt likes to play **basketball**.

86

MAKING WORDS

20 min.

In addition to some themed March lessons, you may want to do some lessons this month that once again focus on the blends. Here are four themed lessons and four more-complex, blend-focussed lessons. It is good to continue to do some easier lessons as the year moves on. Some of your children are just beginning to get a sense of how words work and it is a great ego-booster if they can figure out the secret word occasionally. On the other hand, it is also good to have an occasional tricky lesson—particularly one planned by a leprechaun!

Letters: a c h m r
Make: am ha ham ram arm mar car cram arch harm charm March
Sort for: -am -ar -arm -arch
Transfer Words: farm starch star scram

Letters: i g n p r s
Make: is in pin nip pig rig rip grip grin ring sing spring
Sort for: gr -in -ig -ing -ip
Transfer Words: swing ship chip chin

Letters: a i c k p r t
Make: at pat tap tip trip trap part park pack tack tick trick track Patrick
Sort for: t tr; -at -ap -ip -ack -ick
Transfer Words: flat stack clip chick

Letters: a e e u c h l n p r
Make: pan pal lap clap plan each lean clean plane lunch punch peach reach preach leprechaun
Sort for: cl pl; -an -ap -unch -ean -each
Transfer Words: trap bunch mean teach

Letters: a i g k n s t
Make: sit kit kin tin ski skit skin sink sing king sting stink stain taking skating
Sort for: s k t sk st; -it -in -ing -ink
Transfer Words: spin blink fling spit

Letters: a o b l l n s w
Make: no so sob nab lab saw law low slow snow snob slob slab slaw snowball
Sort for: s n l sn sl; -ab -aw -ob -ow
Transfer Words: crab crow job thaw

Letters: e i d f l n r y
Make: fly fry fed red Fred fled find line life file fine fire fired friend friendly
Sort for: f r l fr fl; -y -ed -ine
Transfer Words: shed shine shy try

Letters: a i c h n p s
Make: nap nip sip sap pin pan span spin snip snap pain Spain spinach
Sort for: s p n sp sn; -ip -in -ap -an -ain
Transfer Words: flip clap clip train

ROUNDING UP THE RHYMES

15 min.

Remember to be on the lookout for text with lots of rhyming words when you are reading aloud to your children or when they are reading a selection during guided reading. Here are the rhyming words rounded up after rereading the first six pages of the delightful book, *One Hungry Monster: A Counting Book in Rhyme*, by Susan Heyboer O'Keefe (Scholastic, 1989).

bed	more	hall	head	rail	rug
fed	door	wall	bed	tail	bug

Here are the same words after rhyming words with different spelling patterns have been thrown out.

bed	hall	rail	rug
fed	wall	tail	bug

Here are the same words along with added transfer words based on the rhyming words and having the same spelling pattern.

bed	hall	rail	rug
fed	wall	tail	bug
shed	small	jail	mug

ASSESSING PROGRESS

You may want to look at some March writing samples and compare them to the January samples. Is the child using the Word Wall and other words displayed in the room to correctly spell most words? Can you read the invented spelling of other words? Is there movement for most children from a letter-by-letter sound-matching strategy to a spelling-pattern strategy? For example, the word **race** spelled **r-a-s-e** shows progression in word knowledge from the letter-by-letter spelling **r-a-s**.

You may also want to assess each student's reading level and his use of word strategies on that level, particularly for each child who was at a beginning-first-grade (or lower) reading level in January. Can the child read a more difficult passage now with word accuracy of 90-95% and with more adequate comprehension than he could two months ago? When reading at that instructional level, do the child's errors demonstrate a use of context and/or beginning-letter sounds? Is the child making some self-corrections? Remember that children will be reading at different levels, but they should all be developing strategies and showing some growth in the difficulty of the text they can read.

APRIL

April is the time to make sure that those students who still need a nudge get the help they need. This month, add the final words to the Word Wall, and then spend some time with your students overlearning the hard four-letter words. Practice those words using the Word Wall follow-up activities that have been described in previous chapters as well as activities related to words found in class books and theme boards.

Spring is a time of new growth, and it will be a time of new literacy growth for your students as you reinforce the skills that have been learned throughout the year. Continue to provide students with activities in which they can have fun learning more about words and discover that they can become better readers and writers.

In April, poetry selections will help solidify all the ways rhyming has been used in Word Walls, On-the-Back activities, Making Words, and Rounding Up the Rhymes.

By this month, there are probably children who know much more about letters, sounds, and spelling patterns than they are actually demonstrating in their everyday reading and writing. Modeling the word strategies and reminding students when they see the strategies will help all children grow into independence and allow them to *apply* what they know.

By the end of April, you will have introduced the following:

- Continued practice of the Word Wall words ("overlearning")
- Extended On-the-Back activities that include rhyming words with endings
- Making Words activities where students find sorting patterns—beginning letters, endings, and rhyming words
- Guess the Covered Word activities which include content from across the curriculum and in which the locations of words in sentences are varied and
- Rounding Up the Rhymes activities that use poetry
- Strategic, decoding- and spelling-coaching strategies that make student learning more explicit

WORD WALL

10 min.

ON-THE-BACK ACTIVITY

20 min.

As April 15th approaches, get ready to pay your income taxes and to put the last word on the wall! Your goal should be to get the last new words on the wall with about six weeks remaining in the school year to review the words (greatly increasing the chances that children will still be able to read and/or spell the words when they return to school in the fall). Remember that although Word Wall is helpful to your fast learners who need some daily practice with handwriting and who profit greatly from the On-the-Back writing activities, Word Wall is most helpful to children for whom learning the abstract, connecting, often-not-spelled-the-way-they-sound words is a huge chore! **Better to put up just over 100 words by mid-April and do lots of practice until the end of the year than to keep adding words which your fast word learners have probably already learned and which you won't have enough time to practice for your struggling students to learn them.**

In addition to learning the words, students need to continue practicing how to spell words with endings and to continue the On-the-Back rhyming activities which help them spell lots of words. Once most children get good at each of these, they can also learn how to do both at one time.

Using Rhyming Words with Endings Added

Begin the combined activity using the easier rhyming format where students find rhyming words for a single Word Wall word. If, for example, the Word Wall word you select is **down**, share the following sentences and have children identify the word in each that rhymes with **down** and has an ending added:

I liked the **clowns** at the circus.

I saw the teacher **frowning** at me.

In the play, I was **crowned** the king.

My brother fell in the pool and almost **drowned**.

I have lived in three different **towns**.

You could also do this with the harder rhyming format where students must choose which of the Word Wall words rhymes with a word in each sentence that has an ending added. Make sure, however, that everyone spells the word aloud correctly before writing it because this could be frustrating for many of your children. If the Word Wall words called out are **tell**, **school**, **but**, **make**, and **rain**, the sentences might be:

My sister won the **spelling** bee.

The **brakes** don't work on my bike.

I **trained** my dog to give me his paw.

I make money **cutting** the grass in my yard.

We stayed at a huge hotel with two **pools**.

MAKING WORDS

20 min.

Children need to look at the words and see patterns and by this time in the year, our questions should be leading them to that kind of independent thinking about the words they see.

In addition to presenting Making Words lessons connected to your themes or units, you may want to continue using Making Words lessons that focus children's attention on the blends. Here are some lessons to help you do that. **Remember that when you have students sort the words, they should first sort for the beginning letters, then for endings (if there are any), and finally for rhymes.** By using this order you will end up with the rhyming words lined up one under another so that they can be used to read and spell a few new words. **Also remember that the *children* should be finding the patterns.** Early in the year, we would get the children to sort by saying things like:

> "Who can go up and find the two words that begin with **dr**?"

> "Who can go up and find the words with the **ing** endings?"

> "Who can go up and find all the words with the **ag** spelling pattern?"

By now we would say:

> "Who can go up and sort the words by the beginning letters in front of the vowel?"

> "Who can go up and find some words with the same endings?"

> "Who can go up and sort the words into rhymes with the same spelling pattern?"

More Making Words Lessons:

Letters: a o d g n r s
Make: go do dog rag ran Dan rod road roan drag drags grand groan groans dragons
Sort for: d r g dr gr; -an -ag -oan
Transfer Words: flag clan moan plan

Letters: e o f l r s w
Make: so sow low for few flew flow slow slew lower slower flower flowers
Sort for: s l f fl sl; low/lower; slow/slower; -ow -ew
Transfer Words: show threw chew glow

Letters: a i f h r s s t
Make: sit hit his tar sir stir star sash sift shift shirt stash stairs starfish
Sort for: s h t st sh; -it -ift -ash
Transfer Words: cash gift smash split

Letters: e i l p p r s y
Make: spy sly sir sip lip slip lips pies lies pile pipe spire slipper slippery
Sort for: s l p sp sl; -y -ip -ies
Transfer Words: ties chip shy cries

92

GUESS THE COVERED WORD

20 min.

You don't always have to use the names of your children in Guess the Covered Word activities. Perhaps you want to write some sentences with connections to your theme/unit. **April is also a good time to have some covered words in various positions in the sentences. Be sure children read the whole sentence (skipping over the covered word when it is in the beginning or middle of the sentence) before they give their guesses.**

Here are some sentences with a seasonal focus and with the target words in various locations in the sentences:

Plants

Seeds **travel** in the wind and in the water.

Sometime animals **move** seeds to other places.

Plants need soil, light and water in order to **grow**.

We can eat the **stems** of some plants.

The roots, seeds and leaves of many plants are **delicious**.

Springtime

April brings lots of springtime **rainy** weather.

All those showers make lots of colorful flowers **bloom**.

It's fun to play **baseball** on a warm spring day.

Going **fishing** is my favorite thing to do this time of year.

My Dog Cleo

Cleo loves to go for walks around the **neighborhood**.

Chasing a ball in the yard is Cleo's favorite game.

Cleo will beg and roll over for a **juicy** bone.

Cleo eats rice and **hamburger** for her dinner.

Our Field Trip

Visiting the **firefighters** was a lot of fun.

While we were at the **station**, the alarm went off.

Firefighters **raced** to get dressed in boots, pants, and helmets.

Sirens and flashing lights warn everyone to get out of the way.

ROUNDING UP THE RHYMES

🕐 15 min.

Poems are wonderful candidates for Rounding up the Rhymes. Children enjoy the silliness of the rhyme, "Cinderella."

> Cinderella, dressed in yellow
> Went upstairs to kiss her fellow.
> Got the sweetest kisses yet.
> How many kisses did she get?
> One, two, three...
>
> Cinderella, dressed in red,
> Went downstairs to bake some bread.
> Cindy's bread was sweet as cake.
> How many loaves did she bake?
> One, two, three...
>
> Cinderella, dressed in blue,
> Went outside to tie her shoe.
> She was only half awake,
> How many hours did it take?
> One, two, three...

This poem was taken from *The Big Book of Playground Rhymes & Chants,* (Evan-Moor Publishers, 1993).

Here are the rhyming words rounded up and written on index cards:

yellow	yet	red	cake	blue
fellow	get	bread	bake	shoe
			awake	
			take	

Here are the words left after discarding the rhymes with different spelling patterns:

yellow	yet	cake
fellow	get	bake
		awake
		take

Here is what the pocket chart looked like at the end of the lesson with transfer words added:

yellow	yet	cake
fellow	get	bake
bellow	wet	awake
		take
		make

As in Making Words lessons, *you* decide what the transfer words will be rather than asking children to give words that rhyme to avoid getting words that rhyme but have different spelling patterns. Children are aware that words with different spelling patterns can rhyme because they see rhyming pairs such as polite/sight and said/head before you throw them away, but you want them to begin spelling words by pattern rather than letter-by-letter. The first-grader who spells **neat n-e-e-t** is in a more advanced spelling stage than if he used the letter-by-letter spelling **n-e-t**.

Once children get good at spelling by patterns, teach them to use a visual checking system or dictionary to determine which spelling pattern is correct, but this practice is not generally something we would do with first graders.

94

ASSESSING PROGRESS

Coaching for Strategic Decoding and Spelling

If you are like most first-grade teachers in April, you probably have children who know a lot more about letters, sounds, and spelling patterns than they actually use when they are reading and writing. **Throughout this book, we have included reminders to children (and to you!) that the work your students are doing with words is only useful and worthwhile if they are actually using what they know while they are reading and writing.**

The sentences that you have been using in the On-the-Back Word Wall activities have been similar to the ones students would actually be writing, because the goal is to show them how Word Wall words can help them spell lots of other words. In Guess the Covered Word activities, the emphasis has been to help children use meaning, all the beginning letters, and word length when guessing words. By ending each and every Making Words and Rounding Up the Rhymes lesson with a few transfer words that the rhyming words will help students read and spell, you are constantly reminding children how and when to use their word strategies.

In spite of all this concerted effort, there may be some children who participate and seem to understand the word activities, but don't use what they know when they read and write! There are two ways to help children use more of what they know.

Conferencing with Students– Coaching during Writing

The first opportunity occurs during writing conferences when you are helping children fix their spelling on pieces they are going to publish. **In first grade, much of what children write stays in first-draft form and their invented spellings are applauded. When students publish a book or prepare pieces for display on the bulletin board, however, you should help them to spell the words correctly so that other people can read what they wrote.** There are many words which children use in their writing which they can't be expected to know how to spell, and when you conference with them, simply acknowledge the good efforts shown in their invented spellings and then write the correct spelling above each. **There are other situations (such as the misspelling of a word that has a familiar spelling pattern) when you should use the editing conference to teach students and to nudge them forward in their use of spelling patterns.**

Imagine that you are editing with a child at this time of the year and the child has written the word **trade** as **trd**. Ask that child:

> "Where's your vowel? Every word needs at least one vowel. Remember the way that every word we make in Making Words always uses at least one red letter. Stretch out the word **trade** and listen for the vowel you hear."

When the child says he hears the **a**, help him decide where to put it. Add the **e** to the end of the word and tell him that you can't hear the **e** but that if you say **trade** slowly, you can hear the **a** and that when he is trying to spell a word to remember that every word needs at least one vowel.

Now imagine that another child comes to you with **trade** spelled **trad**. You might say something like:

> "That was a good try on **trade**. You wrote down every sound you heard. But lets look at the spelling pattern **a-d**. We know some **a-d** words. **B-a-d** spells **bad**; **m-a-d** spells **mad**; **d-a-d** spells **dad**. Can you think of a word that rhymes with **trade** and use that spelling pattern?"

If **made** is on the Word Wall, the child will probably realize that **trade** should be spelled with the same pattern. It is also possible (but not likely) that he will think of **paid** and want to spell **trade t-r-a-i-d**. In this case, point out that **trade** does rhyme with **paid** and could be spelled like **paid** but point out the other pattern in words like **made** and **grade**.

Editing conferences are a great opportunity for you to individualize what you teach children. For some children, you may want to simply praise the invented spelling efforts and fix the spelling. For other children, you can use the opportunity to point out things about letters, sounds and spelling patterns that they know when doing words but are not applying as they are writing.

Conferencing with Students– Coaching during Reading

The second way to assist children to use what they know while they are reading is to conduct some short (10-12 minutes) individual or very-small-group coaching sessions. Your instruction will be most effective if you lead them through the steps to read a new word at the exact moment they encounter the word. Use text which the students haven't read before and which is going to contain some words they need to figure out. Having text at instructional level (5-10 errors per 100 words) is ideal. Explain to the children that the book will have words they haven't learned yet and that the purpose of these lessons is to see how good readers figure out words they don't know. Have a child begin reading and when the child comes to a word and stops, say:

> "Put your finger on the word and say all the letters."

A good reader looks at all the letters in the word he is trying to read. A child who is struggling with reading tends to look quickly at the word and, if he doesn't instantly recognize it, he may stop and wait for someone to tell him the word. Asking the child to say all the letters forces him to look at all the letters. Sometimes, after saying all the letters, the child may correctly pronounce the word! This is proof that he isn't in the habit of looking at all the letters and you should let him know what he has done by saying something like:

> "That's right. There are lots of words we see when we are reading that we don't recognize right away, but when we look at all the letters, we can sometimes figure them out. Good job! Continue reading."

If, after saying the letters, the child does not say the word, you should say:

"Keep your finger on that word and finish the sentence."

It may seem foolish to have the child keep his finger there but young children's print tracking skills are not nearly as good as ours. Many children can't use the context of the sentence and the letters in the unknown word to figure out a word because once they get to the end of the sentence, they can't quickly look back and find the troublesome word. **Keeping one finger on the word allows the child to quickly track back.** If, after finishing the sentence, the child correctly pronounces the word, say:

"Right. You can figure out lots of words you don't know if you use your finger to keep track of where the word is, finish the sentence, and then do like we do in Guess the Covered Word and guess a word that makes sense, begins with all the right letters and is the right length. Continue reading."

If the child still does not get the word, you have three possible cues to point out. If there is a good **picture clue** (which the child has ignored!), focus attention with a question. You could say:

"What animal do you see in the picture that begins with **l**?'

If the troublesome word can be decoded based on one of the patterns on the Word Wall or used frequently during other word activities, you could say:

"Let's see. The word is spelled **s-t-r-i-n-g**. We know that **t-h-i-n-g** spells **thing**. Can you make this word rhyme with **thing**?

If there is nothing in the picture to help and the word is not easily decodable based on a familiar rhyming word, **you can give an explicit context clue**. Imagine that the troublesome word is **place** in the sentence:

Clifford wanted to go to a faraway place.

You could say:

"Where do you think Clifford might want to go to that begins with **p-l**?"

If the child gets the word after you give the most appropriate cue, be sure to tell the child what he did.

"Right. Lots of times there is something in the picture that matches a word we don't know and if we use the picture and the letters and making sense, we can figure out the word."

Or:

"Right. You can use words that rhyme with words you know to help you figure out lots of words just like we do on the back of our Word Wall paper and when we figure out new words at the end of Making Words or Rounding Up the Rhymes."

Or:

"Right. When you thought about where Clifford might go and the sound for the letters **p-l**, place was a word with the right beginning letters that made sense."

The cueing described so far will let a struggling reader figure out a troublesome word in about 90% of the cases. There will still be occasions when the child will not be able to figure out the word, and if you tell him the word, you are reinforcing the child's "wait and I will be told eventually" decoding strategy. For this reason **you should never tell children the word. Instead, when all else has failed, you can give the child a choice from which he can't fail to get the word.** Imagine that the word is **ridiculous** in the sentence:

That is a ridiculous hat.

Say to the child:

"Well, Let's see. Do you think it says 'That is a **ripe** hat' or 'That is a **ridiculous** hat'?"

The alternative begins with the correct letters but is so unmeaningful that the child will make the right choice. You can then say:

"Good. That was a hard word but you got it! Let's continue reading."

Explaining this in writing makes it sound much longer and more complicated than it actually is.

When you are coaching a child to learn to use what he knows (but isn't using), choose text in which the child is going to come to an unknown word every second or third sentence.

When the child stops at a word, use the following Coaching Steps:

Coaching Steps

1. Have the child put his finger on the word and say all the letters.

2. Have the child keep his finger there and finish the sentence.

3. Say, "What do you see in the picture that starts with—?"
   or
   "This word is spelled —. We can spell —. Can you make this rhyme with —?"
   or
   "Where do you think — would go that starts with ?"

4. Finally, if all above cueing fails, say, "Let's see. Do you think it says, 'That is a (**ridiculous** hat),' or, 'That is a (**ripe** hat)'?"

When the child gets the word after any of your cueing, congratulate him and point out what strategy he used that helped him figure out the word.

If a child miscalls a word (instead of the usual struggling reader strategy of stopping on the word and waiting to be told), wait for the child to finish the sentence and then repeat the sentence as the child read it. Point out that it didn't make sense and then take the child through as many steps as necessary.

Most children do not need the kind of one-on-one or very-small-group coaching described here, but for those who do, short coaching sessions held a few times each week make a world of difference in their ability to use what they know when they need to use it!

Summer is coming, and with it comes warm weather (or hot weather in some places!). Hopefully, the hard work that you have done throughout the year has made students "hot" on reading and writing.

The end-of-the-year writing that students do, which often includes stories about mother (for Mother's Day) or informational reports about flowers or plants (if you choose plants as a class theme), should include Word Wall words that are **all** to be spelled correctly.

By this time in the school year, see how many students can spell unknown words using the correct spelling patterns by "reading the room." Some children can self-edit and peer-edit, and almost all students have favorite books and authors.

First grade is a magic year. The proof is sitting in your class. Listen to them read; look at your students write. The activities during these final months help you see that all your hard work has paid off!

By the end of the school year, you will have introduced the following:

- Review of the Word Wall words with some new twists–a new ending **er** and riddles to explore opposites
- Be-a-Mind-Reader format where you watch students scan Word Wall words based on a variety of clues
- Continued coaching of reading strategies so that they become an automatic part of the students' thinking while decoding and spelling
- Making Words activities that include less-frequently encountered letters (**j, q, x, z**), the three sounds of **y** (yes, dry, rusty), and the names of the days of the week

- Guess the Covered Word activities using chosen paragraphs or text from books that are read to the children
- Rounding Up the Rhymes activities that use words from real books
- Creation of a class book with Hink Pinks—rhyming pairs like **damp camp**

WORD WALL

15 min.

The Word Wall activities for May and June should focus on reviewing word endings and spelling patterns for all the words already on the Word Wall. Continue working with the important **s**, **ed**, and **ing** endings and perhaps show students how they can add **y** to words on the Word Wall like **jump**, **rain**, and **fun** to spell **jumpy**, **rainy**, and **funny**. You could also show how to add **ly** to words like **nice** and **friend** to make **nicely** and **friendly**. You can add **er** and **est** to **new**, **little** and **pretty**. **Talk**, **jump**, **kick**, **ride**, **make**, **eat**, and **quit** can each name the person who performs the action by adding **er**. Continue working with both rhyming formats to help students leave first grade understanding that rhyming words usually have the same spelling pattern and to encourage students to use words they can spell to spell lots of other rhyming words.

ON-THE-BACK ACTIVITY

20 min.

Opposite Riddles

By now your Word Wall should have a good number of words that have opposites. Challenge the students to identify each word by presenting a Word Wall "riddle," where the clue you give is the word that means the opposite of the Word Wall word you want students to identify. For example:

Word number one begins with the letter **p** and is the opposite of **ugly**.

Word number two begins with the letter **g** and is the opposite of **bad**.

Word number three begins with the letter **d** and is the opposite of **up**.

Word number four begins with the letter **l** and is the opposite of **big**.

Word number five begins with the letter **b** and is the opposite of **worst**.

ON-THE-BACK ACTIVITY

20 min.

Be a Mind Reader

Of all Word-Wall review activities, this may become the children's favorite. In Be a Mind Reader, you pick one word and you give five clues. The children number their papers from 1-5 as always, but this time they are trying to guess the word you have chosen. Give five clues to the word you have chosen and let students write a guess after each clue is given. If a new clue confirms a student's previous guess, he can write the same word on the line that matches the new clue number. As you progress to the fifth clue, the word which you have in mind should become more obvious. By the last clue everyone should have the word. But who read the teacher's mind and got it on the fourth clue? the third? the second? or maybe even the first clue?

Here are some clues for a Be a Mind Reader activity. All the first-grade words listed on page 30 would be on the Word Wall. Give the clues one at a time and allow each student time to make a guess and write it on his paper.

1. It is one of the words on the wall. (This is always the first clue.)

2. It has four letters. (This eliminates a whole lot of words—but there are still a lot of possible words.)

3. It begins with the letter w. (Now we're narrowing it down, but which one?)

4. It ends with a t. (Well, it's either <u>went,</u> <u>what</u>, <u>won't</u> or <u>want</u>, but which one?)

5. It makes sense in the sentence: I _____ to the mall.

Now everyone has **went** on the last line, but who read my mind? Raise your hand if you had **went** on line 4. (Lots of hands) Raise your hand if you had **went** on line 3. (A few hands) Raise your hand if you had **went** on line 2. (Usually a hand) Raise your hand if you had **went** on line 1. (Miraculously, given the odds every once in a while someone guesses the one word from all the Word Wall words that the teacher was thinking of. That child read her mind!)

MAKING WORDS

20 min.

There are many possibilities for Making Words lessons as the year draws to a close. The first four lessons listed on this page review some of the blends. The next four lessons use the letters **j**, **q**, **x**, and **z** (if, for no other reason than to use those letter cards at least once!). The last seven lessons are fun lessons and can help review the spelling of the days of the week. Do them in any order you choose and watch to see how many days it takes before students catch on that the secret word is one of the days of the week!

Be sure to review the rule that important names like names of people and names of days of the week begin with capital letters. Many teachers like to have the letter **y** card be a different color from all the rest of the letters. It can't be the same color as either the consonants or the vowels, because sometimes it is a consonant and sometimes it is a vowel! In addition to the usual things to sort for, lessons containing **y** words are sorted for the three sounds of **y** as in **yes**, **dry**, and **rusty**.

More Making Words Lessons

Letters: e i u b b d l r
Make: red bed bid lid led bled bred bird blue blur ride bride bridle bluebird
Sort for: r l b bl br; -ed -id -ide
Transfer Words: wide grid sled pride

Letters: a e i c l n r t
Make: car cat rat rate late lane cane lean clean clear crate crane clarinet
Sort for: c l r cr cl; -at -ane -ate -ean
Transfer Words: ties chip shy cries

Letters: a e l p r s y
Make: lap rap Ray pay pry pray play leap plea layer relay replay player plyers players
Sort for: p l r pr pl; -ap -ay
Transfer Words: slap strap stray spray

Letters: a o o b f l l t
Make: lab lob lot bat fat flat flab foot fool fall ball blot bloat float football
Sort for: b l f fl bl; -at -ab -all -ot -oat
Transfer Words: brat slot goat small

Letters: a e c j k s t
Make: at sat set jet Jack tack sack Jake cake take Kate skate stack jackets
Sort for: j; -at -et -ack -ake
Transfer Words: shake pet snake snack

Letters: a e u q r r s t
Make: at eat ear tear rust rest test quest quart stare squat square arrest quarters
Sort for: qu squ; -ear -est -are
Transfer Words: spare chest spear share

Letters: e e i n s t x
Make: in is it sit six nix ten teen seen next exit exits exist sixteen
Sort for: words with x; -it -ix -een
Transfer Words: fix green grit mix

Letters: i o o g m n z
Make: in on no go goo moo zoo zoom zing moon goon oozing mooing zooming
Sort for: ing endings; -o -oo -oon
Transfer Words: boo yo soon spoon

Letters: a u d n s y
Make: us as ad an Dan and sun sad say day any sand sandy Sunday
Sort for: sand/sandy -ay -an -ad -and
Transfer Words: spray bran brand glad

Letters: a o d m n y
Make: on an am dam yam day Dan Don any man mad May many moan Monday
Sort for: -ay -an -am -on
Transfer Words: clay clan clam stray

Letters: a e u d s t y
Make: yes yet tea eat use used stay seat east easy yeast study stayed Tuesday
Sort for: ed pairs; y-yes, yet yeast; easy, study; -eat -east
Transfer Words: feast beat beast treat

Letters: a e e d d n s w y
Make: sad dad end Ned wed dew new news weed need deed seed send ended Wednesday
Sort for: end/ended, new/news; -ad -ed -eed -end -ew
Transfer Words: speed flew threw drew

Letters: a u d h r s t y
Make: try dry shy art dart hard yard tray stay dash trash study sturdy Thursday
Sort for: st, tr; y-try, dry, shy/duty, study, sturdy; -art -ard -ash -ay -y
Transfer Words: card cry smash smart

Letters: a i d f r y
Make: if day Ray dry fry far fir air fair fairy dairy diary Friday
Sort for: f fr; y-fry, dry/fairy, dairy, diary; -ay -air -y
Transfer Words: why gray hair pair

Letters: a a u d r s t y
Make: at sat rat try dry duty dust rust rusty dusty study sturdy Saturday
Sort for: s st; y-try, dry/duty, dusty, rusty, study, sturdy; rust-rusty, dust-dusty; at -ust
Transfer Words: just flat bust trust

GUESS THE COVERED WORD

20 min.

Use the months of May and June to consolidate the strategy of looking at all the letters up to the vowel, looking at the length of the word, and thinking of the word that would make sense to decode unknown words. Try to get the children to verbalize the strategy. Ideally, they should all know that:

"When you see a word you don't know, you can usually figure it out if you say **blank** and finish the sentence and then go back and guess a word that has all the right beginning letters and makes sense in the sentence. It also helps to look at how long the word is."

Perhaps you would like to write a paragraph where each sentence has a word to be guessed that is covered with the usual two sticky notes. Read the paragraph one sentence at a time and allow students to make guesses for each covered word. As you progress through the paragraph, students should be using the whole context of what has been read so far to figure out each new covered word. **Be sure to have your sticky notes cut to size so that word length is obvious and when you remove the first one, show them all the letters up to the vowel.**

Here is an example of a paragraph that can be used in your Guess the Covered Word activity where the topic of the paragraph can help students with their word-guessing:

There are many exciting **things** to do in the summer. Some children go to **camp**. Some children go to the **park**. It is also fun to go to the **playground**. When it is hot, you can go **swimming**. You can also cool off by turning on the **sprinkler**. Trips to the **library** or the **mall** are fun. Some people take long trips to the **beach** or to the **mountains**. Some really lucky people go to **the circus**.

Another possibility is to cover some words in big books you are going to read to the children. Use sticky notes to cover each word to be guessed. Have students follow the usual procedure where they guess without seeing any letters and then let them refine their guesses by letting them see all the letters in front of the vowel. Below is an example from *Thinking About Ants,* by Barbara Brenner, (Mondo, 1996).

An ant can live in a house between the cracks in the f□ or behind the kitchen cupboard□□ Even the □ stem of a plant can be □ to an ant.

20

ROUNDING UP THE RHYMES

15 min.

If your children like dinosaurs, they will love the counting book, *Ten Little Dinosaurs*, by Pattie Schnetzler (Accord, 1996). Use the book in Rounding Up the Rhymes lessons for May and June. Remember to read the book once or twice for content before focusing student attention on the rhymes in the text.

Another book you could use for Rounding Up the Rhymes is *My Teacher's My Friend* by P.K. Hallinan (Childrens Press, 1989). After reading the book, you can reflect back over the school year and the things you did each day. Does the teacher in the book have fun with words the way your class does? She might, because on page 20 of the book they are looking at the rhyming words **catch, match, hatch,** and **patch**! Let's hope that that teacher transfers and talks about the words **batch** and **scratch** next!

Read and enjoy the book, then reread the book and write the rhyming words. Here are the words rounded up and written on index cards:

s<u>ay</u>	gr<u>ass</u>	s<u>ong</u>
w<u>ay</u>	cl<u>ass</u>	al<u>ong</u>
<u>hearts</u>	th<u>ere</u>	d<u>ay</u>
p<u>arts</u>	ch<u>air</u>	w<u>ay</u>
sp<u>in</u>	w<u>ays</u>	w<u>eek</u>
beg<u>in</u>	d<u>ays</u>	sp<u>eak</u>
cr<u>ies</u>	adm<u>it</u>	f<u>uss</u>
<u>eyes</u>	f<u>it</u>	b<u>us</u>
<u>end</u>		
fr<u>iend</u>		

Next, look at the spelling patterns in each pair of rhyming words. Here are the words left after discarding the rhymes with different spelling patterns:

s<u>ay</u>	gr<u>ass</u>	s<u>ong</u>
w<u>ay</u>	cl<u>ass</u>	al<u>ong</u>
d<u>ay</u>	sp<u>in</u>	w<u>ays</u>
w<u>ay</u>	beg<u>in</u>	d<u>ays</u>
adm<u>it</u>		
f<u>it</u>		

Here are the words that would be in the pocket chart at the end of the lesson with transfer words added:

s<u>ay</u>	gr<u>ass</u>	s<u>ong</u>
w<u>ay</u>	cl<u>ass</u>	al<u>ong</u>
cl<u>ay</u>	p<u>ass</u>	wr<u>ong</u>
	gl<u>ass</u>	
d<u>ay</u>	sp<u>in</u>	w<u>ays</u>
w<u>ay</u>	beg<u>in</u>	d<u>ays</u>
tr<u>ay</u>	w<u>in</u>	pl<u>ays</u>
adm<u>it</u>		
f<u>it</u>		
h<u>it</u>		
spl<u>it</u>		

HINK PINKS

20 min.

Hink Pinks are rhyming pairs. Children love to illustrate them and to make up and solve riddles for which they are the answers. You will love them because they help children attend to the relationship between spelling patterns and rhymes and because they give children a real purpose for looking for and manipulating rhyming words.

Here are some Hink Pinks to get you and your students started. Consider having the class make a Hink Pink book which can be duplicated so that each student has a copy to take home for the summer.

drab cab	rag bag
brain strain	fake snake
damp camp	thin fin
fine pine	pink drink
bright light	cold gold
long song	rude dude
book crook	broom room
last blast	brave slave
clay tray	weak beak
beast feast	red shed

free bee	hen pen
bent cent	tent rent
wet pet	nice price
crop flop	cross boss
hound sound	mouse house
stout scout	low blow
brown crown	duck truck
fudge judge	glum chum
fun run	tall wall
skunk bunk	dry fly
loose goose	fox box

ASSESSING PROGRESS

Coaching for Strategic Decoding and Spelling

Don't give up! During editing conferences, continue to remind students (as necessary) that every word needs a vowel. If a word has been misspelled (and the misspelling contains a pattern that is familiar to the student), review the word by pointing out what the word would be the way the student has spelled it.

Keep working with individuals or very small groups for short coaching sessions in which you remind students to use what they know when they need to use it. Students may not all be perfect at doing this, but by the time school is out each child should all know that when he comes to a word he doesn't know, he should:

1. Put a finger on the word and say all the letters.

2. Keep the finger there and finish the sentence.

3. Look for something in the picture that starts with the letters.

   or

   Look at how the word is spelled to see if you know another word with the same spelling pattern.

   or

   Decide what word makes sense and begins with the right letters.

End-of-the-Year Assessment

To make an end-of-the-year assessment, you should look at how far students have come. Most teachers repeat whatever assessments they did at the halfway point of the year. Many schools have assessment teams that go to each class and administer Informal Reading Inventories to all children to determine their instructional reading levels.

Information that will be helpful to next year's teacher can be compiled in some kind of growth portfolio. In many schools there are some pieces (focused writing samples, IRI results, developmental spelling tests, etc.) which are included in all portfolios. Individual teachers, and sometimes children, then choose a few additional pieces to represent their growth. A short write-up by the teacher is usually included for each child. This write-up describes the child's literacy early in the year and the growth each child has made.

Children come to us at all different stages of literacy development. Some children develop literacy including decoding and spelling strategies quickly and seemingly effortlessly. Other children take longer and need lots of practice, nudging, and coaching. Assessment which focuses on and documents growth allows to us do the kind of multilevel instruction all classrooms of children need and allows us to celebrate how far each child has come instead of bemoaning the fact that they are not all "on grade level."

Overview: A Balanced Literacy Program in a First-Grade Classroom

This chapter provides an overview of the entire 4-Blocks balanced literacy program of which the phonics and spelling activities described in this book are one component.

Each year, six million children begin school in our public schools. Many of these children can be immediately identified as "at-risk"—the currently popular descriptor for those children who will not learn to read and write well enough to achieve a basic level of literacy and a high school diploma. The number of children at risk varies from community to community and state to state. Nationwide, NAEP results suggest that more than one-third of all nine year olds cannot read at the "basic" level. For African Americans, 61% fail to achieve this basic level (Mullis & Jenkins, 1990).

These statistics have held fairly constant despite decades of expensive attempts to "fix" the problem. Federal fix-ups have generally included a variety of pull-out remediation programs which have spawned huge bureaucracies and have not succeeded in eliminating the risk for very many children. State and local fix-ups often consisted of passing regulations that prohibited children being promoted unless they obtained certain test scores and result in a huge numbers of children being retained. Shepard and Smith (1990) reviewed decades of research on retention. Their data

show that retained children perform more poorly when they go to the next grade than they would if they had been promoted without repeating a grade and that almost any alternative is more effective than retention. Their data also suggest that "transition" classes, when they result in all children in them spending another year in the primary grades, have the same ill effects as retention.

Within individual schools or classrooms, in addition to federally provided remediation and state or locally mandated retention, teachers usually try to meet the needs of at-risk children by putting them in a "bottom" reading group and pacing their instruction more slowly. The data on bottom groups does not hold out much hope that this solution will ultimately solve the problem. Children who are placed in the bottom group in first grade generally remain there throughout their elementary school career and almost never learn to read and write up to grade-level standards (Allington, 1983; Allington, 1991)

Against this backdrop, we have the peculiarly American phenomenon of the "pendulum swing." Various approaches to reading come in and out of fashion. Eight years ago when we began this endeavor, literature- based reading instruction (commonly referred to as "whole language") was the recommended approach.

Today, this approach is losing favor and school boards are mandating phonics approaches and purchasing spelling books. The search for the "best way to teach reading" denies the reality of individual differences. Children do not all learn in the same way and consequently, approaches with particular emphases are apt to result in some children learning to read and others not. When the pendulum swings to another approach, we may pick up some of those who weren't faring too well under the previous emphasis but lose some who were. Thirty years ago, the First-Grade studies which were carried out to determine the best approach concluded that the teacher was more important than the method but that in general combination approaches worked better than any single approach. (Bond & Dykstra, 1967)

This chapter describes the development of a framework for beginning reading instruction that had two goals. The first goal was to avoid the pendulum-swing and not be trendy but rather to find a way to combine the major approaches to reading instruction. The second goal was to meet the needs of children with a wide range of entering literacy levels without putting them in ability groups.

This project began in the fall of 1989 in one first-grade classroom (Cunningham, Hall & Defee, 1991; Hall, Prevatte & Cunningham, 1995) This classroom was one of four first grade classrooms in a large suburban school to which children from the inner city were bussed. The class contained 26 children, half boys and girls, 26% African-American. The teacher was an experienced teacher who agreed to work with us to see if we could come up with a "do-able" classroom framework for meeting the dual goals of (1.) provid-

ing nonability grouped instruction that met the needs of children with a wide range of entering literacy levels, and (2.) providing children with daily instruction incorporating several reading approaches. During this first year, we developed the instructional framework and assessment procedures. At the end of this year, our success propelled us to involve other first grade teachers at three schools. We refined the framework to accommodate the teaching styles of 16 unique first-grade teachers.

In the third year, we continued to work with first-grade teachers and children and expanded the program to second grade. From the fourth year on, we have worked with numerous school districts throughout the country to implement this balanced framework in hundreds of first and second grades.

THE INSTRUCTIONAL FRAMEWORK

The instructional framework is the heart of our program. The basic notions of this framework are quite simple but its implementation is complex. There is a lot of variation depending on how early or late in the year it is and whether the framework is being carried out in first or second grade. There is also much variation attributed to the individual teaching styles of the teacher and the particular makeup of the class being taught. In this section we will describe the instruction and provide some sense of the variety which allows its implementation in a wide range of classrooms.

In order to meet the goal of providing children with a variety of avenues to becoming literate, instructional time is divided fairly evenly between the four major historical approaches to reading instruction. The $2^1/_4$–$2^1/_2$ hours allotted to Language Arts is divided among four blocks—Guided Reading, Self-Selected Reading, Writing, and Working with Words—each of which gets 30-40 minutes.

To meet our second goal of providing for a wide range of literacy levels without ability grouping the children, we make the instruction within each block as multilevel as possible. For each block, we will briefly describe some of the formats, materials, cooperative arrangements, etc. we use to achieve this goal of multilevel instruction.

SHARED/GUIDED READING

In our first several years, we called this the Basal Block because this was the time when the basal reader drove our instruction. In recent years, teachers have branched out to use other materials in addition to or instead of the adopted basal reader. Depending on the time of year, the needs of the class and the personality of the teacher, guided reading lessons are carried out with the system-wide adopted basal, basal readers from previously adopted

series, multiple copies of tradebooks or books from Wright, Rigby or Troll, articles from *My Weekly Reader,* or similar magazines and big books and combinations of these. The purposes of this block are to expose children to a wide range of literature, teach comprehension, and teach children how to read in materials that become increasingly harder. The block usually begins with a discussion led by the teacher to build or review any background knowledge necessary to read the selection. Comprehension strategies are also taught and practiced during this block. The reading is done in a variety of small group, partner and individual formats. After the reading is completed, the whole class is called together to discuss the selection and practice strategies. This block sometimes includes writing in response to reading.

Early in first grade, most of our guided reading time is spent in shared reading of predictable books. Brown Bear, Mrs. Wishy Washy and Hattie the Hen are common visitors and children and teacher read together in a variety of choral, echo and other shared-reading formats. Comprehension activities often include "doing the book" in which children are given roles and become the characters as the rest of the class reads the book. Little books based on the big books are read and reread with partners, then individually or in small groups. Class books and take-home books patterned on the big book can be constructed in shared writing activities. Often the big books read during guided reading are chosen because they fit a theme or unit studied by the class and guided reading time floats seamlessly into other unit-oriented activities. Follow-up activities for the book and theme often occupy some of the afternoon time.

As the year goes on, the shared reading of big books continues to be a part of guided reading—often providing the easier reading half of the grade-level and easier reading we try to provide each week. Other books, not big and not predictable, are added. There books might be part of a basal series or they might be multiple copies of tradebooks. The emphasis shifts from read together to reading with partners or on your own. Instead of reading the selection first to the children, teachers often take children on a picture walk through the book leading the children to name the things in the pictures, make predictions and pointing out a few critical vocabulary words students might encounter difficulty with as they attempt the reading of the selection. Children then attempt the reading of the selection individually, with a partner or in a small flexible group with the teacher or another helper. The class reconvenes, discusses the selection and then sometimes reads it chorally or in some other whole-class format (not round-robin reading, however!). Comprehension strategies are taught and practiced. Predictions made before reading are checked. Story maps and webs are completed.

The next reading of the selection might include a writing activity. This writing activity is also done by some children individually, some with partners and others in a group guided by an adult. Often the next reading is an acting out of the selection, with various children playing different parts as the rest of the class reads or tells the story.

Making the Shared/Guided Reading Block Multilevel

Guided reading is the hardest block to make multilevel. Any selection is going to be too hard for some children and too easy for others. We don't worry anymore about those children for whom grade-level guided reading material is too easy because the other three blocks provide many beyond-grade level opportunities. In addition, our end-of-year results always indicate that students who begin first grade with high literacy levels read well above grade-level.

We do, however, worry about those students for whom grade-level selections are too hard. To make this block meet the needs of children who read below grade level, teachers make a variety of adaptations. Guided reading time is not spent in grade-level material all week. Rather, teachers choose two selections—one grade-level and one easier—to read each week. Each selection is read several times, each time for a different purpose in a different format. Rereading enables children who couldn't read it fluently the first time to achieve fluent reading by the last reading. Children who need help are not left to read by themselves but are supported in a variety of ways. Most teachers use reading partners and teach children how to help their partners rather than do all their reading for them. While some children read the selection by themselves and others read with partners, teachers usually meet with small groups of children. These teacher-supported small groups change on a daily basis and do not include only the low readers.

In addition to the daily guided reading block in which all children are included, many teachers schedule a 10 minute easy reading support group in which very easy books are read and reread. This group of five to six children changes daily. All children are included at least one day each week. Children who need easy reading are included more often, but not every day. One way or another, we try to assure that every child has some guided reading instruction in material at instructional level or easier several days each week. (For other ways to manage the various levels of children during guided reading, see Cunningham & Allington, 1994.)

SELF-SELECTED READING

Historically called individualized reading or personalized reading (Veatch, 1959), many teachers now label their self-selected reading time Reader's Workshop (Routman, 1988). Regardless of what it is called, self-selected reading is that part of a balanced literacy program when children get to choose what they want to read and what parts of their reading they want to respond to. Opportunities are provided for children to share and respond to what is read. Teachers hold individual conferences with children about their books.

In our classrooms, the Self-Selected Reading block includes (and usually begins with) teacher read-aloud. The teacher reads to the children from a wide range of literature. Next, Children read "on their own level" from a variety of books. In some classrooms, the children read at their desks from crates of books which rotate from table to table. Each crate contains a wide range of levels and types of books and children choose books from that

crate. In other classrooms, you will see children reading at a variety of places. In addition to a reading center, many classrooms have a big book center, a magazine center, a class-authored book center, a science center which includes informational books on the current science topic, a center full of books by a particular author being studied, a taped-book listening center, and sometimes even a computer center with a book on CD. At self-selected reading time, children go to these centers. In some classrooms, they rotate through the centers on different days and in other classrooms they choose which center they want to go to.

Regardless of where the children are, classrooms with successful self-selected reading time all rigorously enforce the "No Wandering" rule. Once you get to your spot, you stay there!

A commonly-observed phenomenon in homes where four-year olds have books and someone to read those books to them is what we call pretend reading. Young children want to do all the things the big people can do. They pretend to cook, to drive, to be the mommy or the daddy and they pretend they can read. They do this pretend reading to a younger child or to a stuffed animal and they do it with a book which they have insisted on having read to them over and over until they can "read" the book! (In fact, this insistence on having a favorite book read hundreds of time is probably motivated by their desire to learn to read!)

Another way, young children read books is by reading the pictures. This is usually done with an informational picture book on a topic of great interest to the child. The parent and the child have probably looked at "the airplane book" or "the dinosaurs book" hundreds of time, spending more time talking about the pictures than actually reading the words. In fact, some of these books have wonderful pictures and lots of sophisticated text and parents don't read the text at all, they just lead the child to talk about the pictures.

We teach our early first graders that they are three ways to read. You can "pretend read" by telling the story of a familiar story book. You can "picture read" by looking at a book about real things with lots of pictures and talking about all the things you see in the pictures. And you can read by reading all the words. Early in the year, we model all types of reading and look at books and decide how children at their age would probably read the book.

> "The Gingerbread Man is a book you could pretend read because you know the story so well. Let's practice how you might pretend read it if you choose it for self-selected reading time."

> "How would you read this book about trucks? It's got lots and lots of words in little tiny print but you could read it by picture reading. Let's practice picture reading."

> "Now, here is an alphabet book. You see just one word and it goes with the picture. You can probably read this book by reading the words."

Once children know there are three ways to read books, no child ever says, "I can't read yet!"

While the children read, the teacher holds individual conferences with children. Most

teachers designate the children as Monday, Tuesday, Wednesday, etc. and then conference with them on their day, spending three or four minutes with each child. Children know that on their day, they should bring one book which they have selected to share with the teacher. They read (in whichever of the three ways is appropriate for that book) a few pages to the teacher and discuss the book and why they chose it. Thus each child gets a short but dependable conference time with the teacher each week to share what they like about books.

Making the Self-Selected Reading Block Multilevel

Self-selected reading is, by definition, multi-level. The component of self-selected reading that makes it multilevel is the fact that children choose what they want to read. These choices, however, can be limited by what reading materials are available and how willing and able children are to read from the available resources. Fielding and Roller (1992) sum up the problem many struggling readers have with self-selected reading:

> While most of the children are quiet, engaged, and reading during independent reading times, there are always a few children who are not. They are picking up spilled crayons, sweeping up shavings from the pencil sharpener, making trips to the water fountain, walking back and forth alongside bookcases, opening and closing books, and gazing at pictures. (p.678)

The article goes on to indicate that many of the children who "wander round" during self-selected reading time are the ones whose reading ability is limited and concludes that:

Either they do not know how to find a book that they can read, or there is no book available that they can read or they do not want to read the books they can read. These children remind us of Groucho Marx: They refuse to become a member of any club that will accept them. In book terms, they cannot read the books they want to read and they do not want to read the books they can read. (p.679)

Fielding and Roller go on to make excellent and practical suggestions about how to support children in reading books they want to read which, without support, would be too difficult and how to make the reading of easy books both enjoyable and socially acceptable. These suggestions include: Helping children determine when a book is just right; encouraging children to read books which the teacher has read aloud; encouraging children to read with a friend and to do repeated readings of books they enjoy; teacher modeling the enjoyment to be found in easier books; setting up programs in which children read to younger children and thus have a real purpose for engaging easy books; and making lots of informational picture books available. Although they do not use the term, following their suggestions would make the self-selected reading time more multilevel. We have incorporated many of their ideas in our Self-Selected Reading block and in addition we steer our more advanced readers toward books that challenge them.

WRITING

The writing block is carried out in "Writers' Workshop" fashion (Graves, 1994; Routman, 1988; Calkins, 1994) It begins with a 10-minute mini-lesson. The teacher sits at the overhead projector or with a large piece of chart paper. The teacher writes and models all the things writers do (although not all on any one day). The teacher thinks aloud—deciding what to write about and then writes. While writing, the teacher models looking at the Word Wall for a troublesome word which is there as well as inventing the spelling of a few big words. The teacher also makes a few mistakes relating to the items currently on the editor's checklist. When the piece is finished or during the following day's minilesson, the children help the teacher edit the piece for the items on the checklist. Next the children go to their own writing. They are at all different stages of the writing process—finishing a story, starting a new story, editing, illustrating, etc. While the children write, the teacher conferences with individuals who are getting ready to publish. From 3-5 pieces, they choose one to make into a book. This piece is edited with the teacher's help and the child proceeds to the publishing table where he or she will copy the edited piece and finally illustrate the book. This block ends with "author's chair" in which several students each day share work in progress or their published book.

Early in first grade, our writing block begins with what we call "Driting." As with reading, if you observe those lucky preschool children who have things to write with and on and encouragement from parents, they pretend they can write. They do this by combining drawing along with some circle/line-letter-like forms and then some letters, a few words (sometimes copied from a book, sign or calendar) and often a few numbers put in where they "look good." The child then proceeds to "read" what he or she has written, usually to the delight of the parents of this precocious four-year old.

Believing that we must begin where children are and knowing that many of our first graders have not done this driting—drawing and writing—at home, we begin our first-grade writing block with driting. For the minilesson, the teacher places a large sheet of drawing paper on the board and then using crayons, the teacher draws a picture and writes a few words to go with the picture.

"Each day at this time, I am going to draw and write something I want to tell you. Today I am drawing a pizza because today is Thursday and on Thursday night, we don't cook at my house. We go out to eat and each week, we all take turns picking the restaurant. This Thursday is David's night to pick and I know we will be going to Pizza Hut™."

As the teacher is saying this, she is drawing a pizza and writing the words, PIZZA HUT™. In the writing minilesson, we try to model a type of writing which most of our children can achieve. Next, the teacher gives everyone a piece of drawing paper and tells them to

"Use your crayons to draw something you want to tell us. You can write some words too like I wrote PIZZA HUT™ but you don't have to. Draw and write in whatever way you would like so that you can tell us what you want to tell us. It doesn't have to

be about food. It can be about a pet, or what you like to do, or baseball or anything that you want to tell. I am going to give you ten minutes to draw and write and then we will all make a circle and tell about our driting."

As the children draw and write, the teacher goes around and encourages them, responding enthusiastically to whatever they are creating. At the end of ten minutes, the teacher says something like,

"Let's all get in a circle now and anyone who wants to can tell us about their driting. If you have more details you want to add, you can do that later when you have a few minutes of spare time. It doesn't have to be finished for you to tell us about it."

The teacher and children then spend 10-15 minutes, letting volunteers show and tell about their driting.

When we work with teachers, they always ask an unanswerable question: "How long do you stay in the driting stage?" In some classrooms, where most children have been writing in kindergarten or at home, our writing block looks like that described above for only a few days. In other first grades in which the children have had few experiences with print, driting is the writing block variation for several weeks. To answer the question of when to move to the next stage, you have to look at what the children are producing. Each day, when the teacher is doing the driting minilesson, she both draws and writes. Usually, early in the year, most of the children just draw. But, as time passes, more and more children start adding words to their drawings.

Remember—there are three other blocks going on. Words are being added to the Word Wall. Children are learning about letters and sounds as they make words, round up rhymes, guess covered-words, and do other words block activities. Children are having daily guided/shared reading time, and they are reading in whatever way they can during self-selected reading time.

When almost all the children are using both words and drawing in their driting, it is time to move to the next stage. In most classrooms, that move is signalled by a new kind of paper, which has drawing space on the upper half and a few writing lines on the bottom half. Thus, we often call this stage the half-and-half stage.

When the teacher decides it is time to move to the next stage, she begins her minilesson by putting a piece of half-and half paper on the board (or a half-and-half-transparency on the overhead). She says something like,

> "You are learning to read and write so many words that staring today we are going to use this writing and drawing paper for our writing. You will still write and draw what you want to tell us but you can do your writing here and use your pencil and then you can draw your picture here with your crayons. The teacher then models this procedure. She writes a simple sentence or two (Not more!) modelling how to look at the Word Wall for words you know are there and stretching out to invent spell the other words. Then she draws a picture that goes with the writing.

Next the children do their writing and (if you have timed the move correctly) most children write a few sentences. The teacher goes around and encourages and, if asked to spell a word, does not spell, but rather helps the child stretch the word out and get down some letters. After 10-15 minutes, the children circle up and share their creations just as they have been in the driting stage. The teacher responds positively to what they tell, including to those few children who only have a picture! In a few weeks, with the help of the Word Wall and other words around the room and with the teacher to help them stretch out words, even the struggling children will generally write a sentence or two to go with their pictures.

The next move is from the half-and-half stage to the stage in which children are writing on their own without teacher encouragement/ stretching out words. The teacher can now spend the 15-20 minutes when the children are writing to help children revise, edit and pub-lish pieces. This is also the time when we begin to use the author's chair procedure in which the Monday children share on Monday one piece they have written since last Monday, the Tuesday children on Tuesday, etc.

Making the Writing Block Multilevel

Writing is the most multilevel block because it is not limited by the availability or acceptabil-ity of appropriate books. If teachers allow children to choose their own topics, accept whatever level of first-draft writing each child can accomplish, and allow them to work on their pieces as many days as needed, all children can succeed in writing. One of the major tenets of process writing is that children should choose their own topic. When children decide what they will write about, they write about something of particular interest to them and consequently something that they know about. Now this may seem like belaboring the obvious but it is a crucial component in making process writing multilevel. When everyone writes about the same topic, the different levels of children's knowledge and writing ability become painfully obvious.

In one of our classrooms, recently, two boys followed each other in the Author's Chair. Todd, a very advanced writer, read a book he had authored titled *Rocks*. His 16 page-book contained illustrations and detailed descriptions of metamorphic, igneous and sedimentary rocks. The next author was Joey, one of the struggling readers and writers in the classroom. He proudly read his eight-page illustrated book titled *My New Bike*. Listening to the two boys read, the difference in their literacy level was striking. Later, several of the children were individually asked what they liked about the two pieces and how they were different. The children replied that "Todd wrote about rocks and Joey wrote about his bike." Opinions about the pieces were divided but most children seemed to prefer the bike piece to the rock piece—bikes being of greater interest than rocks to most young children!

In addition to teacher acceptance, children choosing their own topics, and not expecting finished pieces each day, Writer's Workshops include two teaching opportunities which promote the multilevelness of process writing—minilessons and publishing conferences. In minilessons, the teacher writes and the children get to watch her thinking. In these daily short lessons, teachers show all aspects of the writing process. They model topic selection, planning, writing, revising and editing and they write on a variety of topics in a variety of different forms. Some days they write short pieces. Other days, they begin a piece that takes several days to complete. When doing a longer piece, they model how you reread what you wrote previously in order to pick up your train of thought and continue writing. The minilesson contributes to making process writing multilevel when the teacher includes all different facets of the writing process, writes on a variety of topics in a variety of forms and intentionally writes some shorter easier pieces and some more involved longer pieces.

Another opportunity for meeting the various needs and levels of children comes in the publishing conference. In some classrooms as children develop in their writing, children do some peer revising/editing and then come to the teacher "editor-in-chief" for some final revision/editing before publishing. As teachers help children publish the piece they have chosen, they have the opportunity to truly "individualize" their teaching. Looking at the writing of the child usually reveals both what the child needs to move forward and what the child is ready to understand. The editing conference provides the "teachable moment" in which both advanced and struggling writers can be nudged forward in their literacy development.

Finally, writing is multilevel because for some children writing is their best avenue to becoming readers. Decades ago, Russell Stauffer (1970) advocated language experience as an approach to teaching reading in which children found success because they could both read their own words (language) and comprehend their own experiences. When children who are struggling with reading write about their own experiences and then read it back (even if no one else can read it!), they are using their own language and experiences to become readers. Often these children who struggle with even the simplest material during guided reading can read everything in their writing notebook or folder. When children are writing, some children are really working on becoming better writers; others are engaging in the same activity, but for them, writing is how they figure out reading.

WORKING WITH WORDS

In the Working with Words block—which is the focus of this book, children learn to read and spell high-frequency words and learn the patterns which allow them to decode and spell lots of words. The first 10 minutes of this block are usually given to reviewing the Word Wall words. The remaining 20-25 minutes of words time is given to an activity which helps children learn to decode and spell words. A variety of different activities are used on different days. Three of the most popular activities are: Guess the Covered Word, Making Words, and Rounding Up the Rhymes. Other activities include: Tongue Twisters, On-the-Back activities, Hink Pinks.

Making the Working with Words Block Multilevel

Throughout this book, we have described how the Working with Words activities are multi-level.

CONNECTIONS ACROSS THE BLOCKS

So far, we have been describing the blocks as separate entities. In most primary classrooms, they each have their allotted time and you can tell when you watch which block the teacher and children are in. As much as possible, teachers try to make connections from one block to another. Many teachers take a theme-approach to teaching. These teachers often select books for guided reading which correlate with their theme. During the writing minilesson when the teacher models writing, he or she often (but not every day) writes something connected to the theme. Some of the books teachers read aloud at the beginning of self-selected reading and some of the books children can choose from are theme connected.

Theme words are not put on the Word Wall—which we reserve for high-frequency words and words that represent high frequency patterns. But most teachers have a theme board or chart in addition to the Word Wall. This board changes with each theme and in addition to pictures includes theme-related words which children will need as they pursue that theme. Often the secret word in a making words lesson is theme connected. Sometimes, the sentences a teacher writes for a Guess the Covered Word lesson relate to the theme.

In addition to theme connections, there are other connections across the blocks. We practice Word Wall words during the words block but we select them once they have been introduced in guided reading and we make sure that the children know that when they are writing, they spell words as best they can unless the word is on the Word Wall. Word Wall words must be spelled correctly!

Rounding up the Rhymes occurs during the words block but the book from which we are rounding has usually been read by the children during guided reading or read aloud by the teacher to begin the self-selected reading block. Sometimes, we do Guess the Covered Word activities by using self-stick notes to cover one word on each page of a big book. We often introduce vocabulary during guided reading through picture walks and while reading with small groups, we coach children on how to decode words using picture, context and letter sound clues.

In our mini-lesson at the beginning of each day's writing time, we model how we can find words we need on the Word Wall and how to stretch out words listening for the sounds to spell big words not available in the room. When we are helping children edit, we praise them for their good attempts and spelling and coach them to use things they are learning during the words block.

Most teachers who have organized their framework within the four-blocks framework find that it is natural and easy to make connections across the blocks. By providing instruction in all four blocks, we provide children with many different ways to learn to read and write. Connections across the blocks help children build bridges between what they are learning.

EFFECTIVENESS OF THE FRAMEWORK

For the last several years, a number of schools and districts have attempted to evaluate the effectiveness of the Four-Blocks Framework. Data is provided from three different sites.

Data from the Original Four-Blocks School

Clemmons Elementary School, where the framework was originally implemented is a large suburban school with a diverse student population. Some children come from homes surrounding the school and others are bussed from the inner city. In any year, 20-25% of children qualify for free or reduced-priced lunches. Approximately 25-30% of the children are African-American, Hispanic or Asian-Pacific Island. Since the program began, the student population has remained relatively stable, with approximately 10% of the children moving in and out each year. There have been three different administrators. Approximately half of the current first and second grade teachers have been there for all six years. The other half, including beginning teachers, have joined the staff during that time. All classes are heterogeneously grouped. Children are not retained, and none are referred for special classes until second grade. The student's population includes all children who are in the school at the end of first and second grade. The majority of the children have had two years of multimethod, multilevel instruction but some children new to the school have had a year or less.

Throughout the year, teachers conduct assessment by observing and conferencing with children, taking running records and looking at writing samples. At the end of the year, children are given the Basic Reading Inventory (Johns, 1997). Instructional levels on the oral reading passages are computed using the standard procedures. Because the IRI is administered at the end of the year, an instructional level of first or second grade is considered grade level at the end of first grade and an instructional level of second or third grade is considered grade level at the end of second grade.

IRI Data is reported starting with our second year in which all first grade teachers were involved and continues through five years of first graders and second graders. Approximately 100-140 children in each grade are included in each year's data.

Across the five years, instructional level results have remained remarkably consistent. At the end of first grade, 58-64% of the children read above grade level—third grade or above; 22-28% read on grade level; 10-17% read below grade level—preprimer or primer. On average, one child each year is unable to meet the instructional level criteria on the preprimer passage. At the end of second grade, the number at grade level is 14-25%. The number above grade level—fourth grade level or above—increases to 68-76% The number reading below grade level drops to 2-9%, half what it was in first grade.

While we have no control group to which we can compare our results, our data was collected across five years and was consistent

across five groups of 100-140 children. The data look remarkably similar even though half the teachers have come since the onset and the school has had several changes in administration. Looking at these data across five years, the most startling (and encouraging) results relate to those children who do not read at grade level at the end of first grade. Out of 100 plus children each year, approximately one child is unable to read the IRI preprimer passage. This child should not be considered a nonreader, however, because this child does have simple predictable books he or she can read and can also read his or her own writing!

Of the 10-15% of children who do not read at grade level at the end of first grade, half are reading on or, in some cases, above grade level at the end of second grade. Looking at the first-grade data, it is impossible to predict which children will make the leap. Some children who read at the preprimer level at the end of first grade read at grade level or above at the end of second grade. Others who read further along—primer level—at the end of first grade only move to first reader level by the end of second grade.

Standardized test data on these children collected in third, fourth and fifth grades each year indicates that 90% of the children are in the top two quartiless. Most years, we have no children whose scores fall in the bottom quartile.

Data from a Suburban School District

The original school in which the framework was implemented does not do standardized testing until the end of third grade. Thus we had to rely on our IRI data to assess the progress of our students. While we feel that IRI data is the best indicator of individual growth in reading, standardized tests have established reliability and are not subject to individual tester bias/skill as IRI's are. We considered the idea of administering standardized tests to all our first and second graders but rejected this notion because of the time and money involved and because we would have no comparable control group. Meanwhile other districts heard about, visited and implemented the framework. Many of these districts did administer standardized reading tests in the primary grades and one district devised an evaluation model, the results of which will be reported here.

Lexington One in Lexington, South Carolina is a suburban southeastern school district with eight elementary schools, in which 25% of the children qualify for free/reduced price lunch. During the 1995-96 school year, first grade teachers in the district were given information about the four-blocks framework and allowed to choose whether or not they wanted to implement the framework in their classrooms. Approximately half of the teachers chose to implement the framework and were provided with several workshops/books and collegial support throughout the year in their classrooms.

In January 1996, 100 first graders in classrooms using the four-blocks framework and 100 first graders in classrooms not using the framework were randomly selected and were given the Word Recognition in Isolation and Word Recognition in Context sections of the Basic Reading Inventory (Johns, 1997). Adjusted means for both measures favored students in the four-blocks classrooms. For the word recognition in context means, the differ-ences were statistically significant. Students in the four-blocks classrooms were on average reading at the beginning of second grade level. Students in the other first grades were on average at the first grade, second month level.

While these results were encouraging, district officials were concerned about lack of reliability on the IRI and about teacher bias, fearing that the enthusiasm of the teachers who chose to implement the model may have created a Hawthorne effect. They then devised an experiment using cohort analysis and standardized test results. In May of 1996, all 557 first graders in four-blocks classrooms were administered the Metropolitan Achievement Test. Each child was matched with a first grader from the previous year (1994-95) based on their scores on the CSAB (Cognitive Skills Assessment Battery), a test of readiness given each year during the first week of school. The total reading mean score for the four-blocks first graders was significantly better (.0001 level) than that of the previous years matched students. In grade equivalent terms, the average four-blocks first grader's total reading was 2.0 while that of the 1994-95 student was 1.6.

Based on the standardized test data, school officials concluded that the four-blocks framework had been much more effective than their previous ability-grouped traditional basal instruction. They hypothesized that since students selected for the cohort group had been taught by all the first grade teachers in the system, teacher bias based on the enthusiasm of teachers choosing to change could not have accounted for the results. Furthermore, their classroom observations suggested that teachers who implemented the four-blocks framework had not all implemented it fully or equally well. In spite of the unequal implementation, with all children in four-blocks classrooms included, they scored on average almost half a year better than the previous group.

This district then analyzed their data by dividing both groups of students into thirds according to their CSAB scores. Children of all ability levels profited from the multilevel four-block instruction. There was a 15 point difference in total reading scores for the lower third, a 23 point difference for the middle third and a 28 point difference for the upper third. The district concluded that organizing in this nonability grouped way had profited the struggling students and had been even more successful for students who would traditionally have been placed in the top group.

Data from One Rural School

During the same year, a nearby school adopted the four-blocks framework and mandated its use in all first and second grade classrooms. Brockington Elementary School in Florence School District Four in Timmonsville, South Carolina is a small rural district in which 84% of students qualify for free/reduced price lunch. Based on low achievement tests scores, the elementary school had been placed on the list of the state's worst schools and had tried a variety of approaches to improving reading and math test scores. During the 1991-92 school year, the school was mandated by a new superintendent to "teach the basics." A state-developed basic skills curriculum focused on "skill and drill" was implemented along with a computer-lab basic skills remediation program for Chapter 1 students. End of the year achievement test scores showed no improvement. During the 1992-93 school year, teachers took a year-long gradu-

ate course on whole language. Again, the end-of-year test results failed to show improvement.

During the 1993-94 school year, another new superintendent arrived. The district continued to emphasize whole language and teachers were trained in cooperative learning. This year's test scores showed some improvement at grades two and three, though none at grade one. During the 1994-95 school year, teachers were urged to continue to use whole language and cooperative learning and they were also trained in Learning Styles approach of Rita Dunn. It is hard to compare test scores for this year because the state changed from the Stanford Achievement Test to the Metropolitan Achievement Test but scores were the worst they had ever been. In grade one, only 20% of the students scored at or above the 50th percentile on total reading. At the second grade level, only 9% scored at or above the 50th percentile.

During the 1995-96 school year, all ten teachers—six at first grade and four at second grade—were trained in and mandated to try the four blocks framework. (It boggles the mind to imagine how enthusiastic and confident these teachers must have been to implement one more "miracle solution!"). These teachers were given workshops/books, state-department, central office support, etc. and in the opinion of those central office and state department facilitators who visited weekly in their classrooms, four of the six first-grade teachers and three of the four second-grade teachers implemented the framework.

MAT total reading scores for all first and second graders in that school (including the three classes which did not really implement the framework) indicated that 30% of the first graders and 38% of the second graders had total reading scores at or above the 50th percentile.

The data from this school system is, of course, open to interpretation. Since different children were tested in the 1994-95 group and we have no pretest data on these children, we cannot be sure that the huge jump in the number of children reading at or above grade level is due to the implementation of the four-blocks framework. Officials in this school district, having tried literally "almost everything" in the previous five years, are convinced, however, that the differences are real and attributable to the balanced multilevel instruction which most of the 1995-96 first and second graders received on a daily basis. They are continuing implementation and eagerly await the results of end-of-year testing.

The last eight years have been exciting and satisfying years for us. We have seen the four blocks framework implemented in hundreds of classrooms in diverse settings, with varied populations of children. This framework has few revolutionary ideas but it provides teachers a way to implement a balanced program and more nearly meet the needs of children with a wide range of levels who do not all learn in the same way.

PROFESSIONAL CITATIONS

Adams, M. J. *Beginning to Read: Thinking and Learning About Print.* Cambridge, MA: MIT Press, 1990.

Allington, R. L. "The Reading Instruction Provided Readers of Differing Reading Ability." *Elementary School Journal, 83,* (1983): 549-559

Allington, R. L. "Effective Literacy Instruction for At-Risk Children." In *Better Schooling for the Children of Poverty: Alternatives to Conventional Wisdom* edited by M. Knapp & P. Shields, 9-30. Berkeley, CA: McCutchan, 1991.

Avery, C. *And with a Light Touch: Learning about Reading, Writing and Teaching with First Graders.* Portsmouth, NH: Heinemann, 1993.

Bond, G. L., & Dykstra, R. "The Cooperative Research Program in First Grade Reading Instruction." *Reading Research Quarterly, 2,* (1967): 5-142.

Calkins, L. M. *The Art of Teaching Writing.* (2nd. ed.). Portsmouth, NH: Heinemann, 1994.

Clay, M. *An Observation Survey of Early Literacy Achievement.* Portsmouth, NH: Heinemann, 1993.

Cunningham, P. M. *Phonics They Use: Words for Reading and Writing.* New York: HarperCollins, 1995.

Cunningham, P. M. & Hall, D. P. *The Four Blocks: A Framework for Reading and Writing in Classrooms that Work.* 1995. This video is available from I.E.S.S. by calling 800-644-5280.

Cunningham, P. M. & Hall, D. P. *Making Words,* Carthage, IL: Good Apple, 1994.

Cunningham, P. M. & Hall, D. P. *Making More Words,* Carthage, IL: Good Apple, 1997.

Cunningham, P. M. & Allington, R. L. *Classrooms that Work: They Can All Read and Write.* New York: HarperCollins, 1994.

Cunningham, P. M., Hall, D. P. & Defee, M. "Nonability Grouped, Multilevel Instruction: A Year in a First Grade Classroom." *Reading Teacher, 33* (1991): 566-571.

DeFord, D. & C. Lyons, S. Pinnell. *Bridges to Literacy: Learning from Reading Recovery.* Portsmouth, NH: Heinemann, 1991.

Fielding, L. & Roller, C. "Making Difficult Books Accessible and Easy Books Acceptable." *The Reading Teacher* 45 (1992): 678-685.

Gentry, J. R. *Spel. . . Is a Four Letter Word.* Portsmouth, NH: Heinemann, 1987.

Gentry, J.R. & Gillet, J.W. *Teaching Kids to Spell.* Portsmouth, NH: Heinemann, 1993.

Graves, D. H. *A Fresh Look at Writing.* Portsmouth, NH. Heinemann, 1994.

Hall, D. P., Prevatte, C. & Cunningham, P. M. "Eliminating Ability Grouping and Reducing Failure in the Primary Grades." In *No Quick Fix,* ed. by R. L. Allington and S. Walmsley, 137-158. Teachers College Press, 1995.

Johns, J. L. *Basic Reading Inventory,* 7th ed. Dubuque, IA: Kendall Hunt, 1997.

Mullis, I. V. S., & Jenkins, L. B. *The Reading Report Card. 1971-88.* Washington, DC: U. S. Department of Education, 1990.

Routman, R. *Transitions.* Portsmouth, NH: Heinemann, 1988.

Routman, R. *Invitations.* Portsmouth, NH: Heinemann, 1994.

Shepard, L. A., & Smith, M. L.. "Synthesis of Research on Grade Retention." *Educational Leadership* 69 (1990): 84-88.

Stauffer, R. G. *The Language-Experience Approach to the Teaching of Reading.* New York: Harper & Row, 1970.

Veatch, J. *Individualizing Your Reading Program; Self-Selection in Action.* NY: Putnam, 1959.

CHILDREN'S BOOKS

The Accidental Zucchini, An Unexpected Alphabet by Max Grover. (Harcourt Brace, 1993).

Alphabet Annie Announces an All-American Album, by Susan Purviance & Marcia O'Shell. (Houghton Mifflin, 1988).

The Alphabet Tale, by Jan Garten. (Random House, 1964).

Animalia, by Graeme Base. (Abrams, 1987).

Ape in a Cape, by Fritz Eichenberg. (Harcourt Brace, 1952).

Are You There, Bear? by Ron Maris. (Puffin, 1986).

The Bear Escape, by Gare Thompson. (Steck-Vaughn, 1997).

The Big Book of Playground Rhymes & Chants. (Evan-Moor, 1993).

The Biggest Sandwich Ever, by Jeffrey Stoodt. (Steck-Vaughn, 1997).

The Biggest Tongue Twister Book in the World, by Gyles Brandeth. (Sterling, 1978).

Busy Buzzing Bumblebees and Other Tongue Twisters, by Alvin Schwartz. (HarperCollins, 1992).

Button Buttons, by Rozanne Lanczac Williams. (Creative Teaching Press, 1994).

Chicka Chicka Boom Boom, by Bill Martin, Jr., & John Archambault. (Simon & Schuster, 1989).

Chicka Chicka Sticka Sticka, by Bill Martin, Jr., & John Archambault. (Simon & Schuster, 1989).

Choose Me! by Sharon Siamon. (Gage, 1987).

Dr. Seuss's ABC, An Amazing Alphabet Book, by Theodore Geisel. (Random House, 1963).

Easy as Pie, by Marcia Folsom & Michael Folsom. (Houghton Mifflin, 1986).

Eating the Alphabet, by Lois Ehlert. (Harcourt Brace, 1989).

Five Little Monkeys. (Mondo, 1995).

Franklin in the Dark, by Paulette Bourgeois. (Scholastic, 1986).

Hattie and the Fox, by Mem Fox. (Simon & Schuster, 1988).

The Hungry Thing, by Jan Slepian & Ann Seidler. (Scholastic, 1988).

I Can Read, by Rozanne Lanczac Williams. (Creative Teaching Press, 1994).

I Can Write, by Rozanne Lanczac Williams. (Creative Teaching Press, 1994).

I Went Walking, by Sue Williams. (Harcourt Brace, 1990).

If You Give a Mouse a Cookie, by Laura Joffe Numeroff. (Harper & Row, 1985).

In a People House, by Theodore LeSieg. (Random House, 1972).

I See Colors, by Rozanne Lanczac Williams. (Creative Teaching Press, 1994).

It Begins with an A, by S. Calmenson. (Hyperion, 1993).

It Didn't Frighten Me, by Janet Goss & Jerome Harste. (Mondo, 1995).

Jake Baked the Cake, by B.G. Hennessey. (Viking, 1990).

Jump, Frog, Jump! by Robert Kalan. (Greenwilow Books, 1981).

Little Red and the Wolf, by Gare Thompson. (Steck-Vaughn, 1997).

My Picture Dictionary, by Diane Snowball & Robyn Green. (Mondo, 1994).

My Teacher's My Friend, by P.K. Hallinan. (Childrens Press, 1989).

Oh No! by Bronwen Scarffe. (Mondo, 1994).

One Fish, Two Fish, Red Fish, Blue Fish, by Theodore Geisel. (Random House, 1960).

On Market Street, by Arnold Lobel. (Greenwillow, 1988).

One Hungry Monster: A Counting Book in Rhyme, by Susan Heyboer O'Keefe. (Scholastic, 1989).

Pretend You're a Cat, by J. Marzollo. (Dial, 1990).

Six Sick Sheep, by Jan Cole. (Morrow, 1993).

Ten Apples Up on Top, by Theodore Geisel. (Random House, 1961).

Ten Little Dinosaurs by Pattie Schnetzler. (Accord, 1996).

There's a Wocket in My Pocket, by Theodore Geisel. (Random House, 1974).

Thinking About Ants, text © 1996, 1986 by Barbara Brenner, illustrations © 1996 by Carol Schwartz. Used by permission of Mondo Publishing, One Plaza Road, Greenvale, N.Y. 11584. All rights reserved.

Time for Bed, by Mem Fox. (Celebration Press, 1993).

Tomorrow's Alphabet, by George Shannon. (William Morrow, 1996).

A Twister of Twists, A Tangler of Tongues, by Alvin Schwartz. (Harper Collins, 1972).

When Goldilocks Went to the House of the Bears. (Mondo, 1995).

When I Grow Up, by Babs Bell Hajdusiewicz. (Dominie Press, 1996).

Where's Spot? by Eric Hill. (Putnam, 1980).

Who Reads? by Betty Aynaga. (Dominie Press, 1996).

Zoo-looking, by Mem Fox. (Mondo, 1995).